continuum

Writer
Stephen Snyder
Sean O'Reilly

Pencils
B.C. Hailes

Colors
Eve

DePasquale

ons   Exec. Administrator
on   **Emma Waddell**

or   General Manager
da   **Michelle Meyers**

ARC
www.ar

ARCA
ALL RIGHTS
The stories, inciden
characters or instituti
review purposes, th

na Studio Inc.
uitlam, BC V3J 2P8.
living or dead or to names,
e exception of cover used for
m without the prior express

ISBN: 978-1-897548-82-0   Printed in Canada

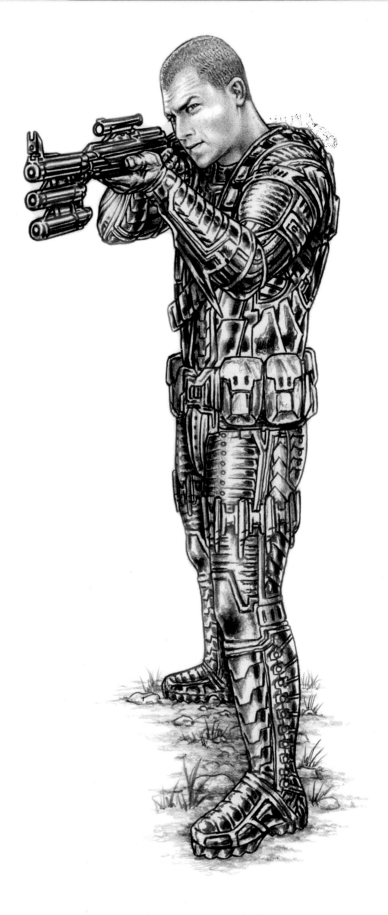

"CPL. DENT"

Chapter One

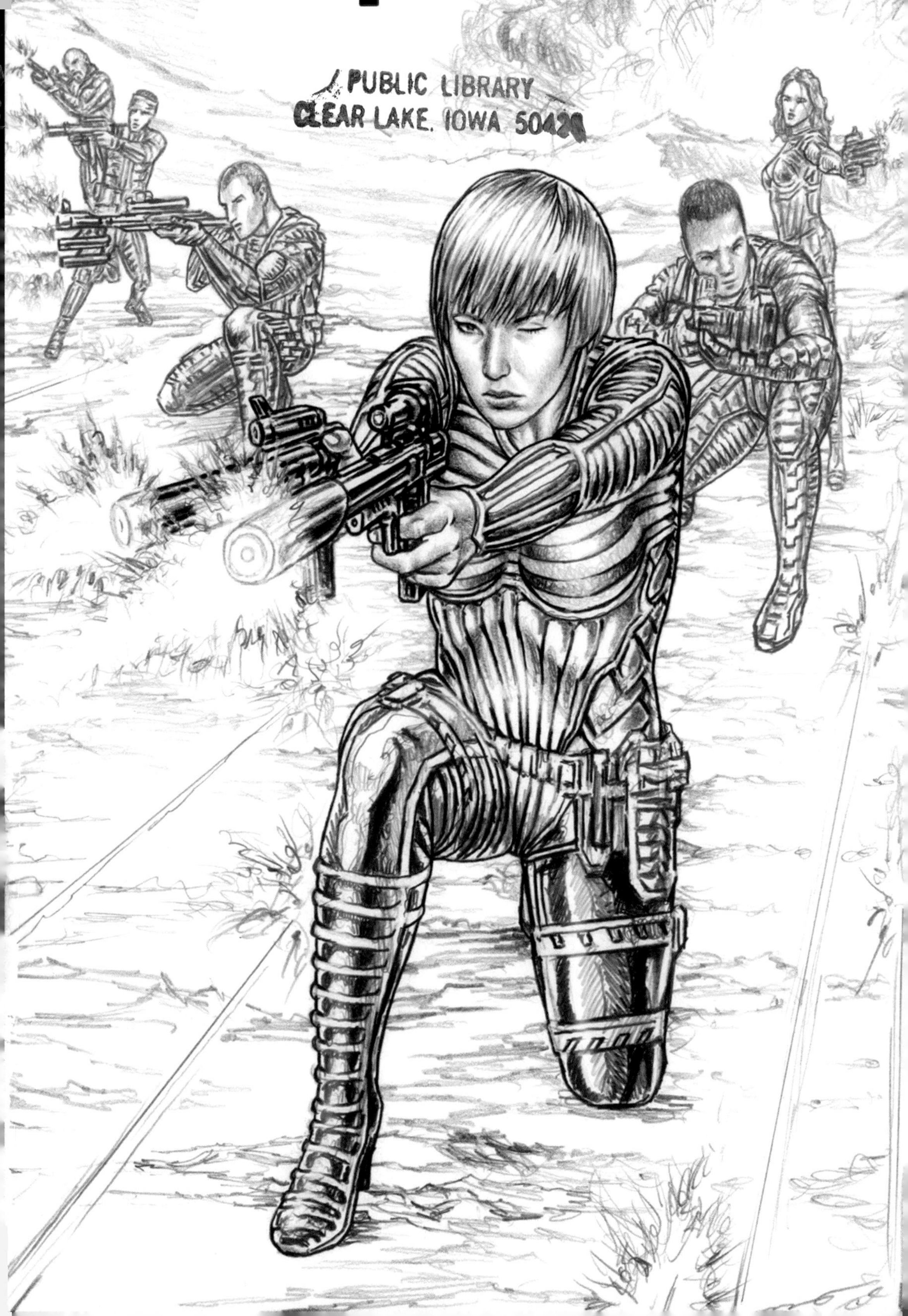

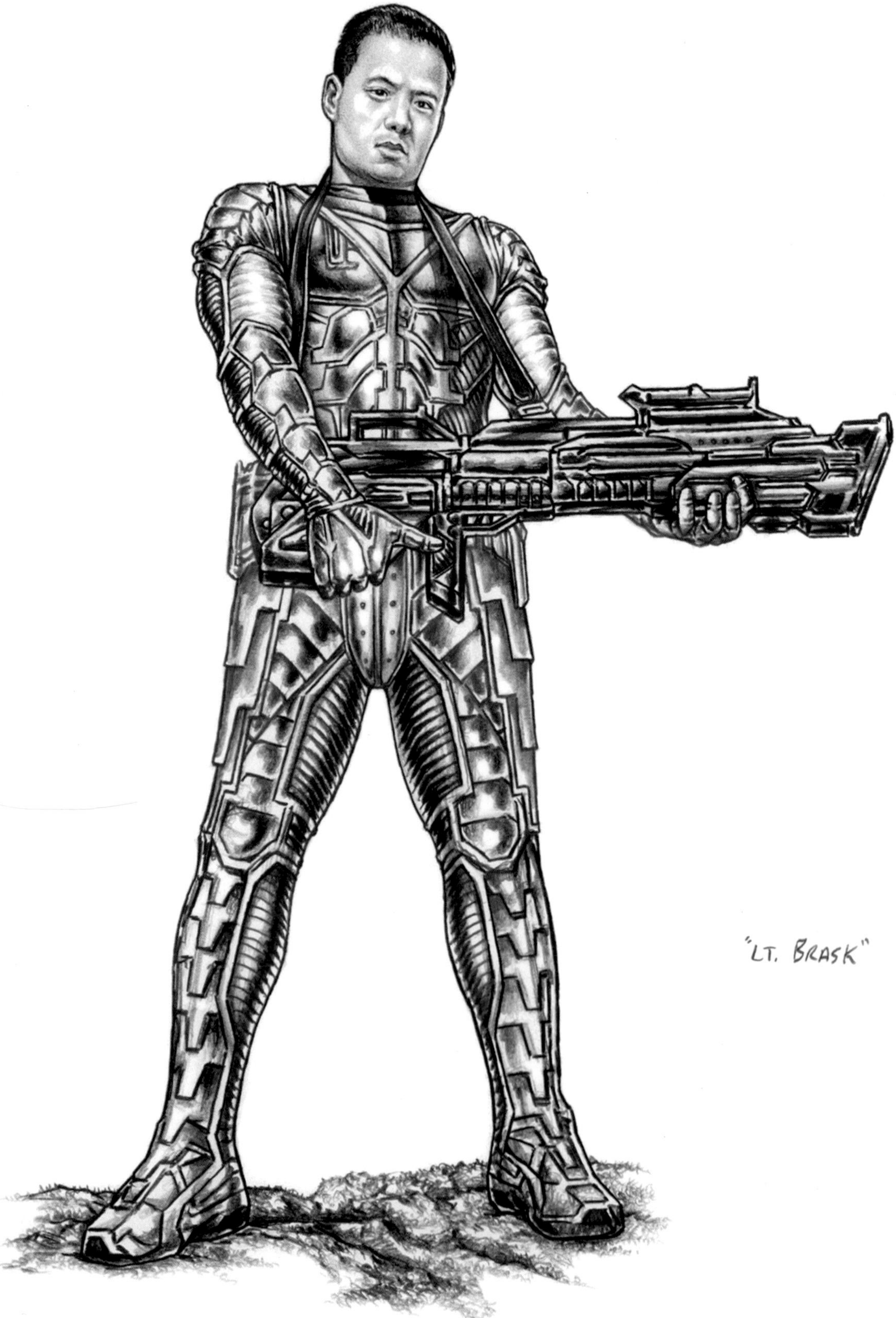

"LT. BRASK"

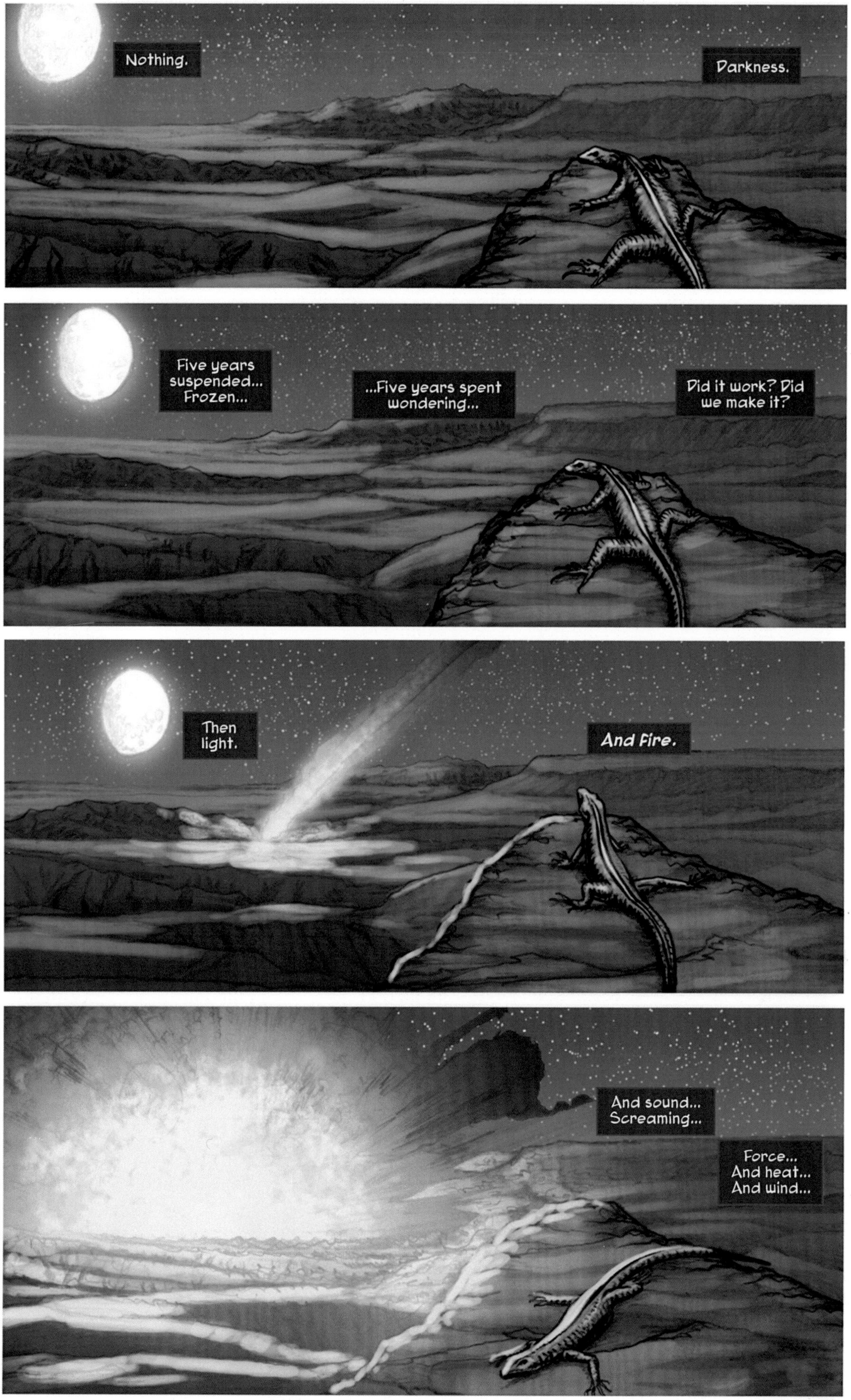
Nothing.
Darkness.
Five years suspended... Frozen...
...Five years spent wondering...
Did it work? Did we make it?
Then light.
And fire.
And sound... Screaming...
Force... And heat... And wind...

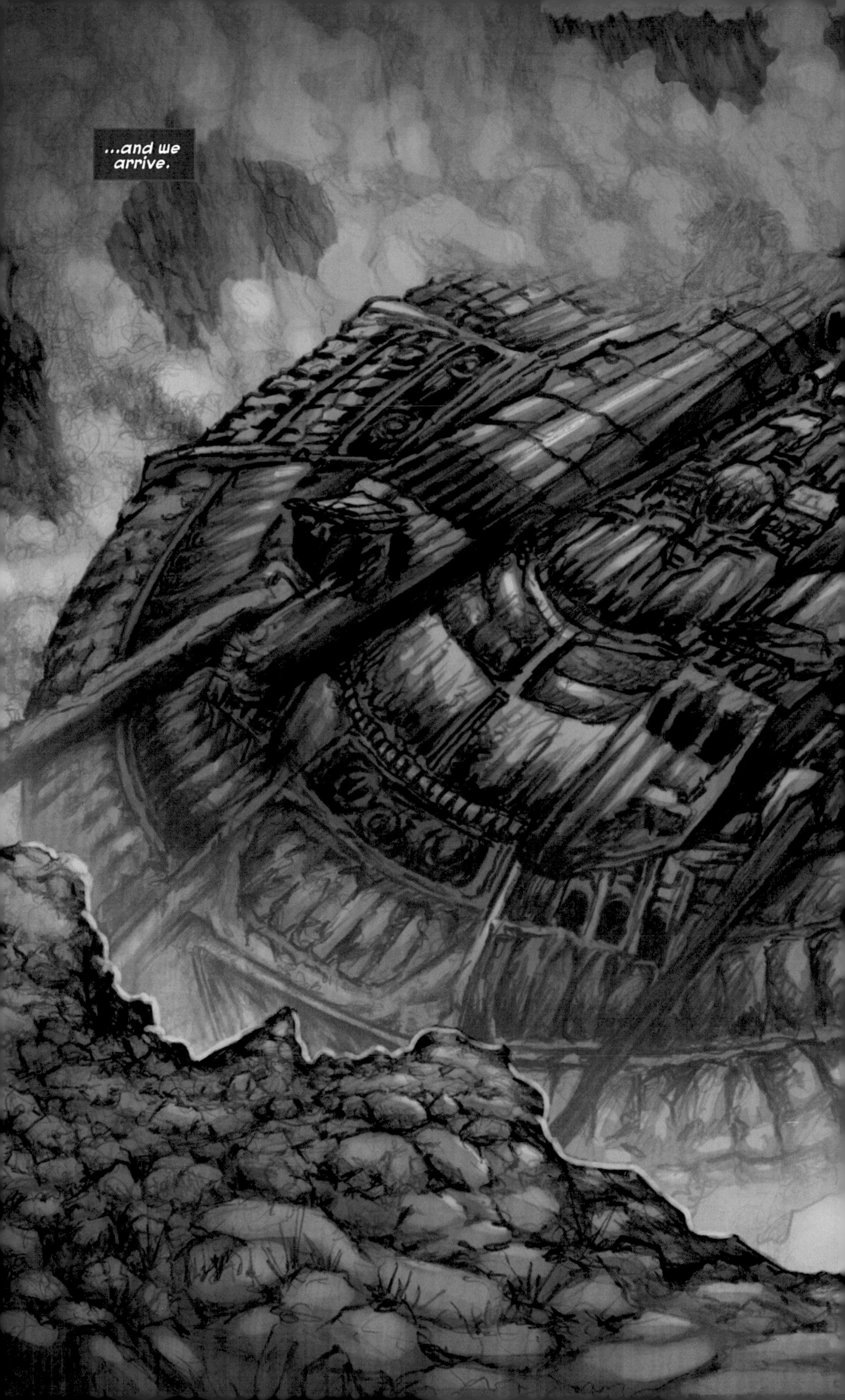
...and we arrive.

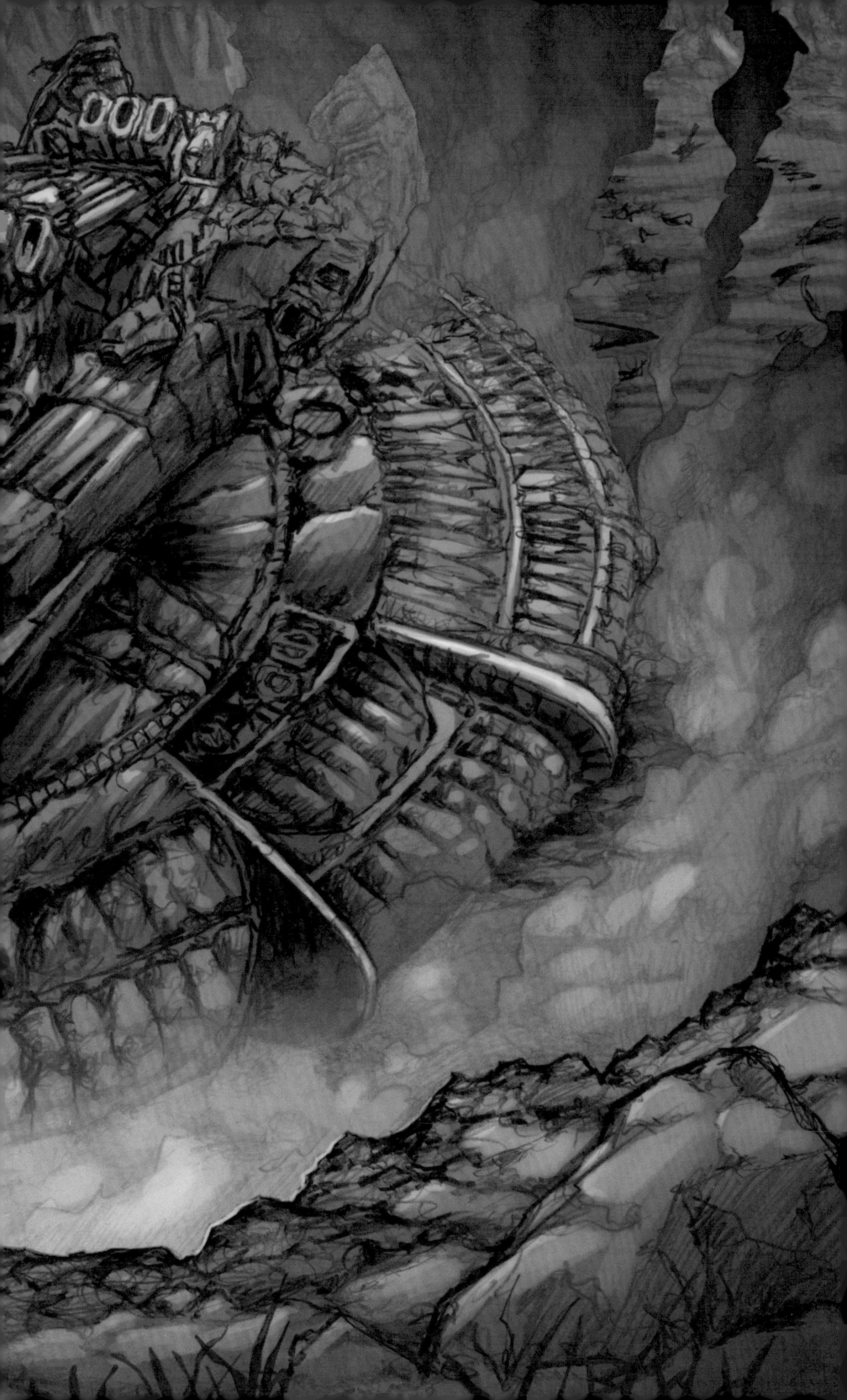

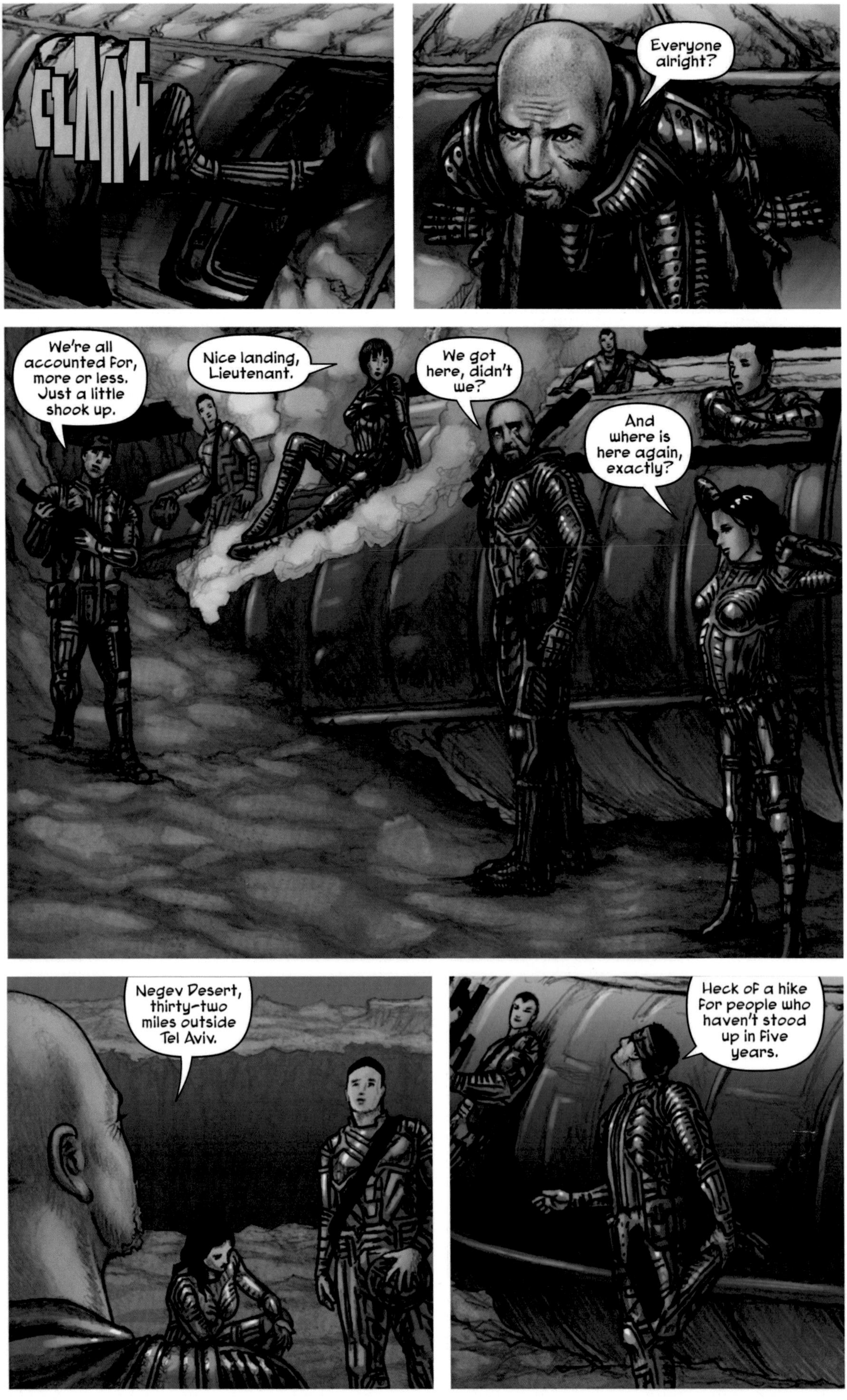
CLANG
Everyone alright?
We're all accounted for, more or less. Just a little shook up.
Nice landing, Lieutenant.
We got here, didn't we?
And where is here again, exactly?
Negev Desert, thirty-two miles outside Tel Aviv.
Heck of a hike for people who haven't stood up in five years.

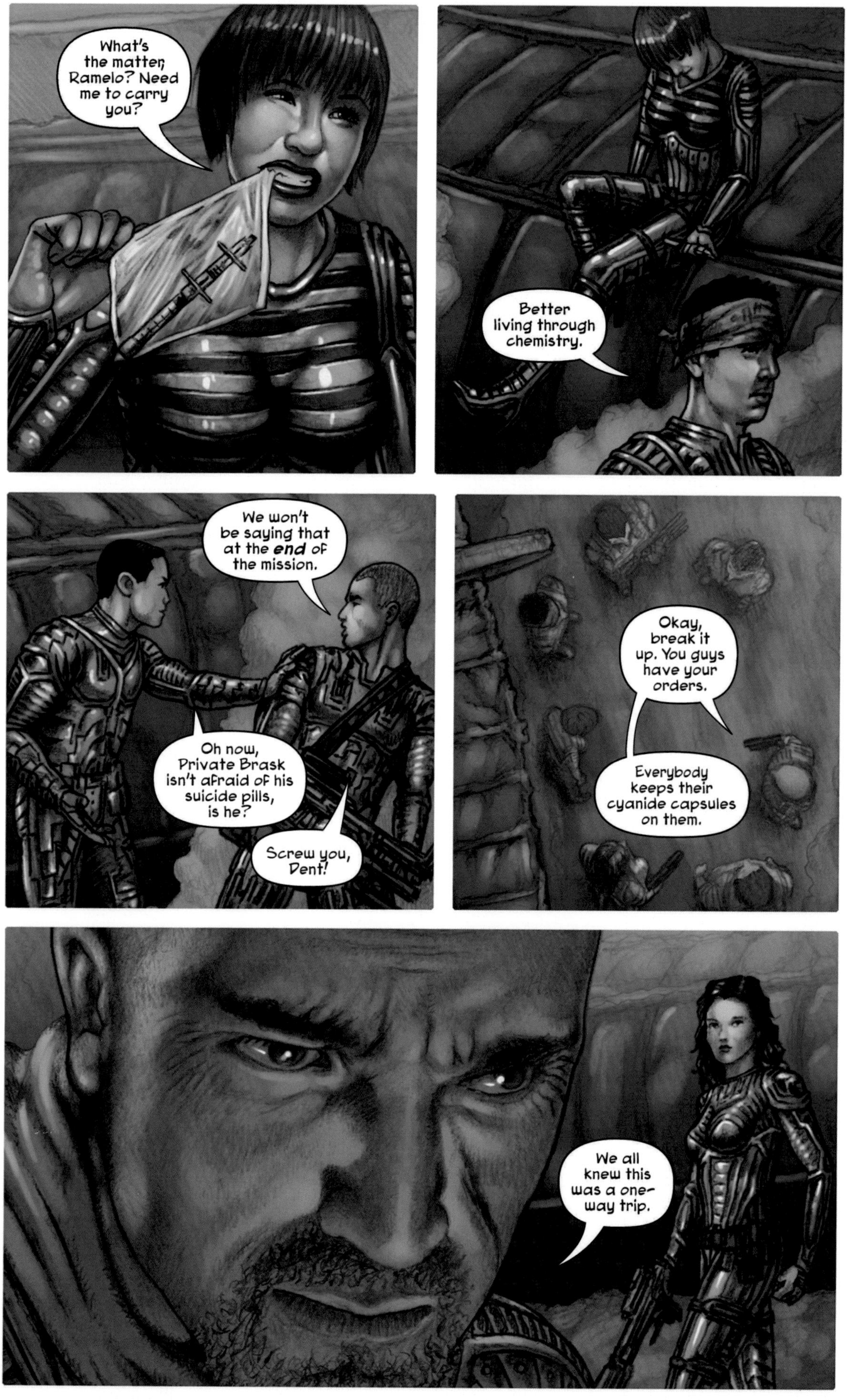
What's the matter, Ramelo? Need me to carry you?
Better living through chemistry.
We won't be saying that at the *end* of the mission.
Oh now, Private Brask isn't afraid of his suicide pills, is he?
Screw you, Dent!
Okay, break it up. You guys have your orders.
Everybody keeps their cyanide capsules on them.
We all knew this was a one-way trip.

Remember, pack only 21st-cen tech. The rest we bury.
I don't want any anachronisms. You hear me, people?
Let's get to work.
You okay, historian?
What? Oh...yeah. I'm fine.
I was just thinking...
Is it possible? Are we really here?
You studied this your entire life, Marcus. Now you get to actually see it...

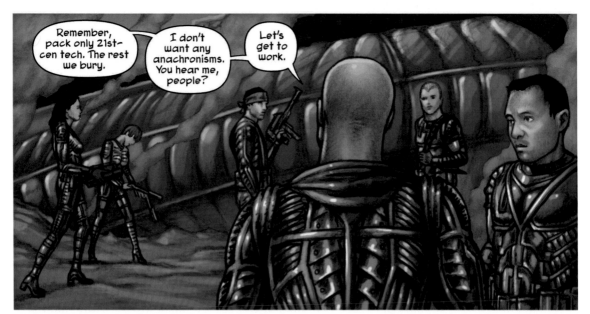

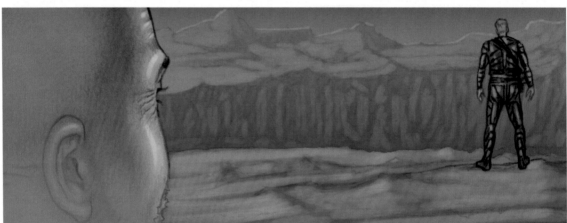

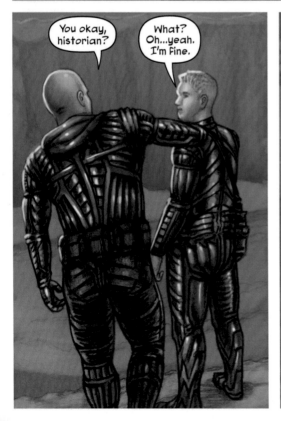

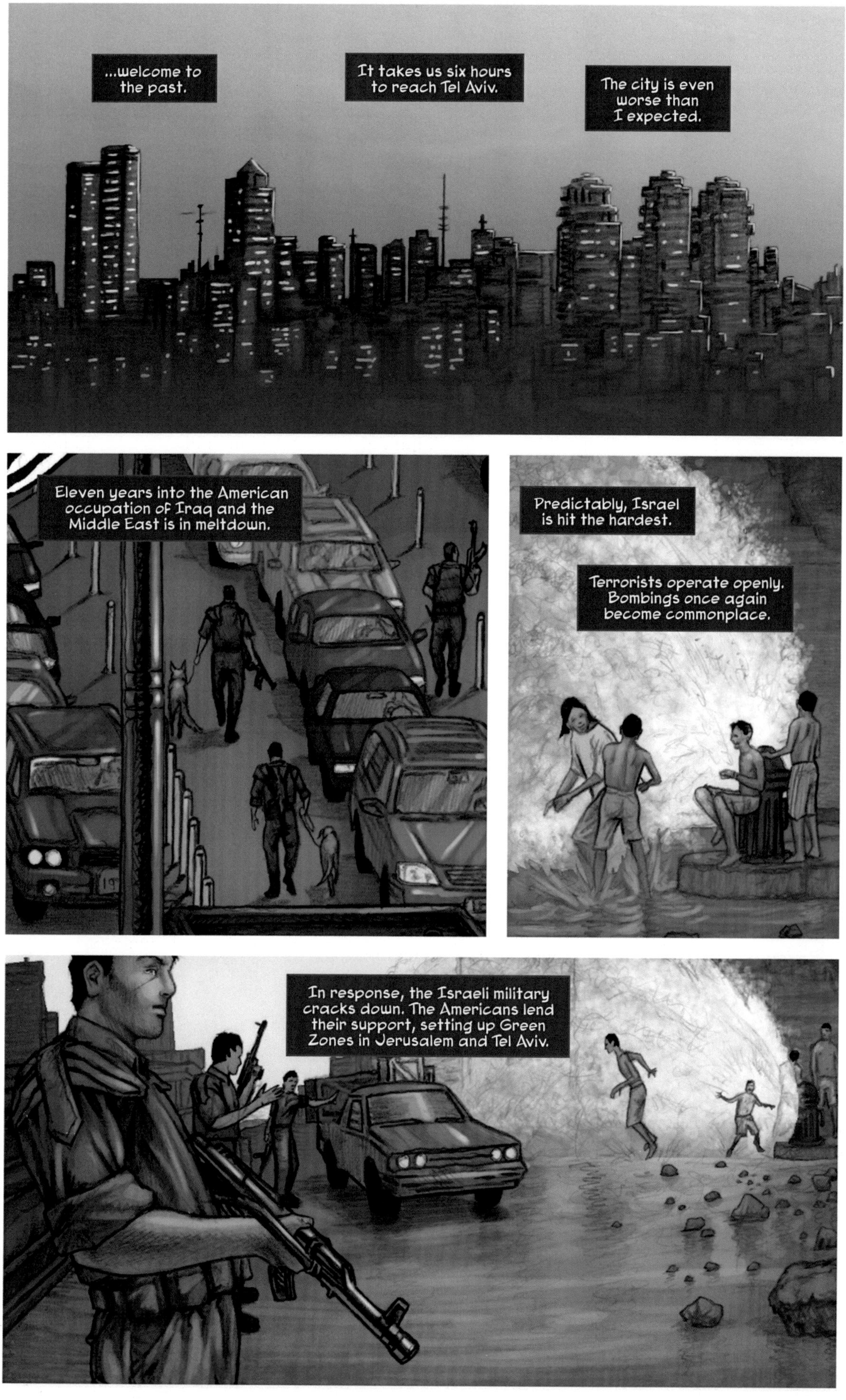
...welcome to the past.
It takes us six hours to reach Tel Aviv.
The city is even worse than I expected.
Eleven years into the American occupation of Iraq and the Middle East is in meltdown.
Predictably, Israel is hit the hardest.
Terrorists operate openly. Bombings once again become commonplace.
In response, the Israeli military cracks down. The Americans lend their support, setting up Green Zones in Jerusalem and Tel Aviv.

Thirty-two hours from now, a young radical name Issa al-Habbas will shoot the Prime Minister of Israel and then detonate a bomb strapped to his chest.

The US and Israel respond by invading Syria – then Iran – in the name of "security."

But all Russia and China see is the oil.

The war that follows is the first using tactical nuclear weapons.

The results are devastating.

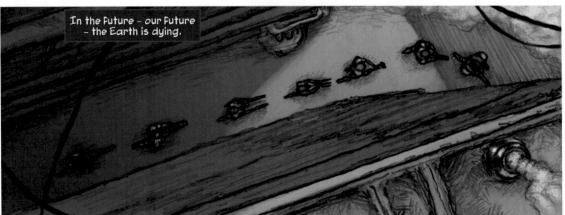

In the future – our future – the Earth is dying.

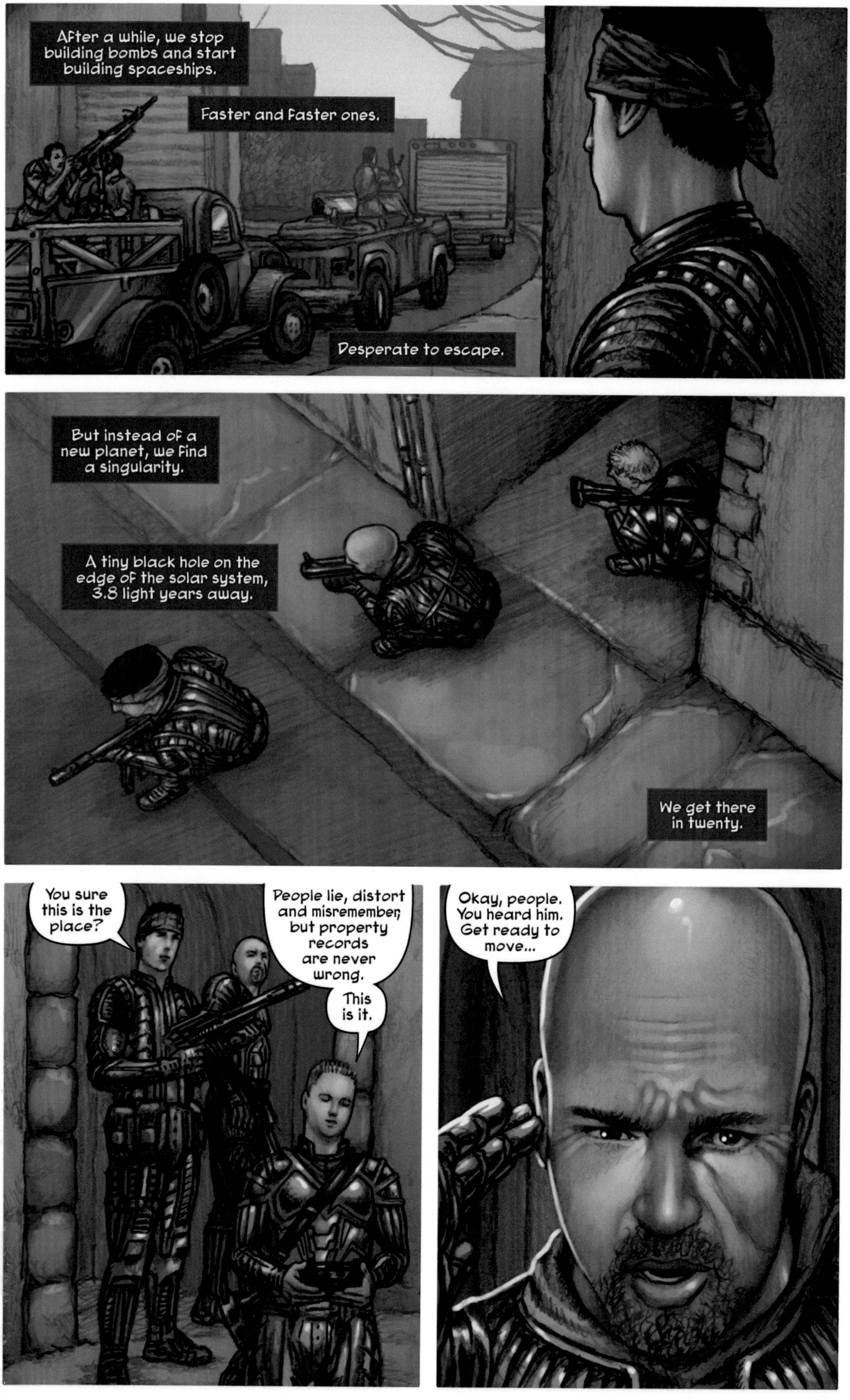

After a while, we stop building bombs and start building spaceships.
Faster and faster ones.
Desperate to escape.
But instead of a new planet, we find a singularity.
A tiny black hole on the edge of the solar system, 3.8 light years away.
We get there in twenty.
You sure this is the place?
People lie, distort and misremember, but property records are never wrong.
This is it.
Okay, people. You heard him. Get ready to move...

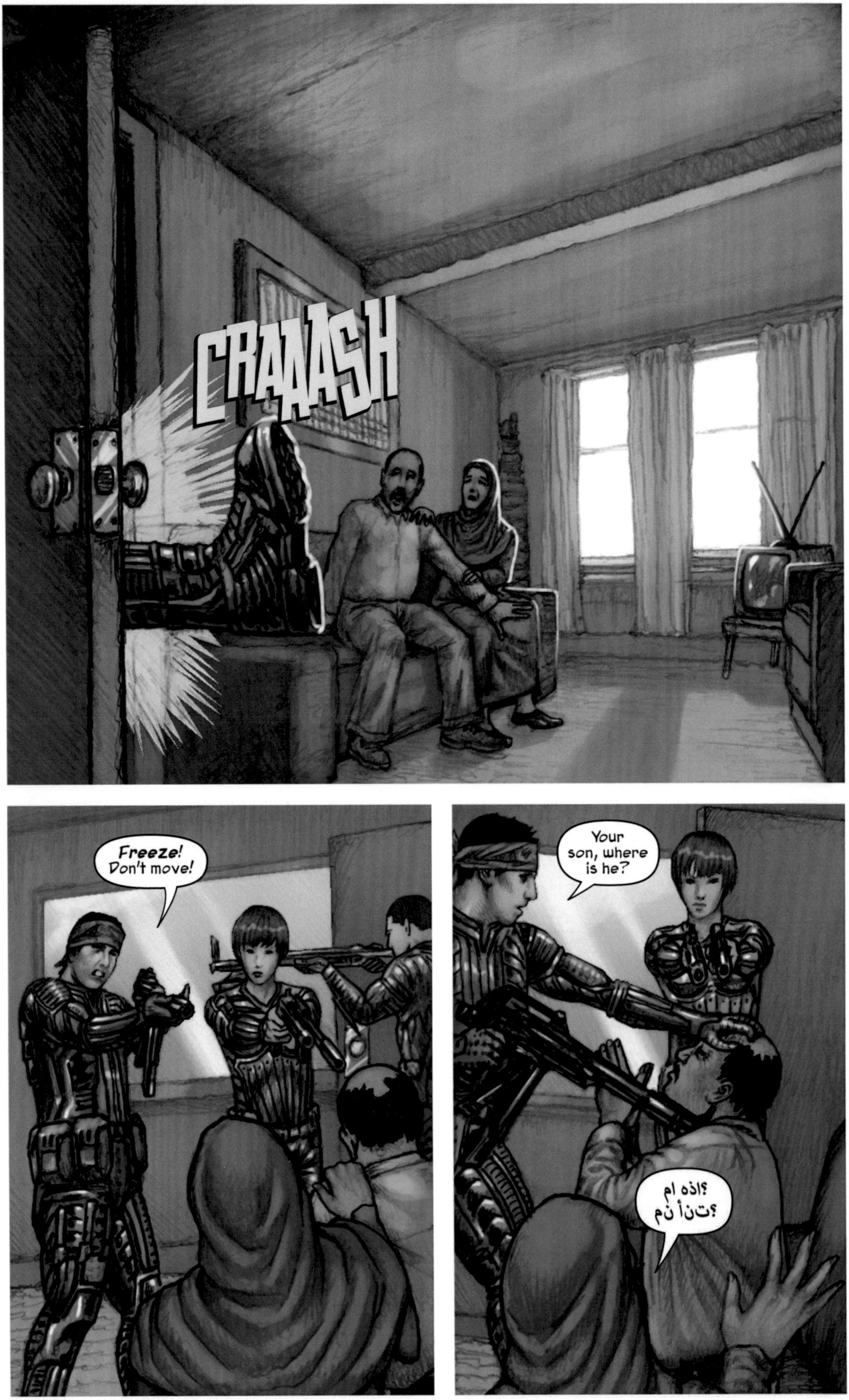
CRAAASH
Freeze! Don't move!
Your son, where is he?
ما هذا؟
من أنت؟

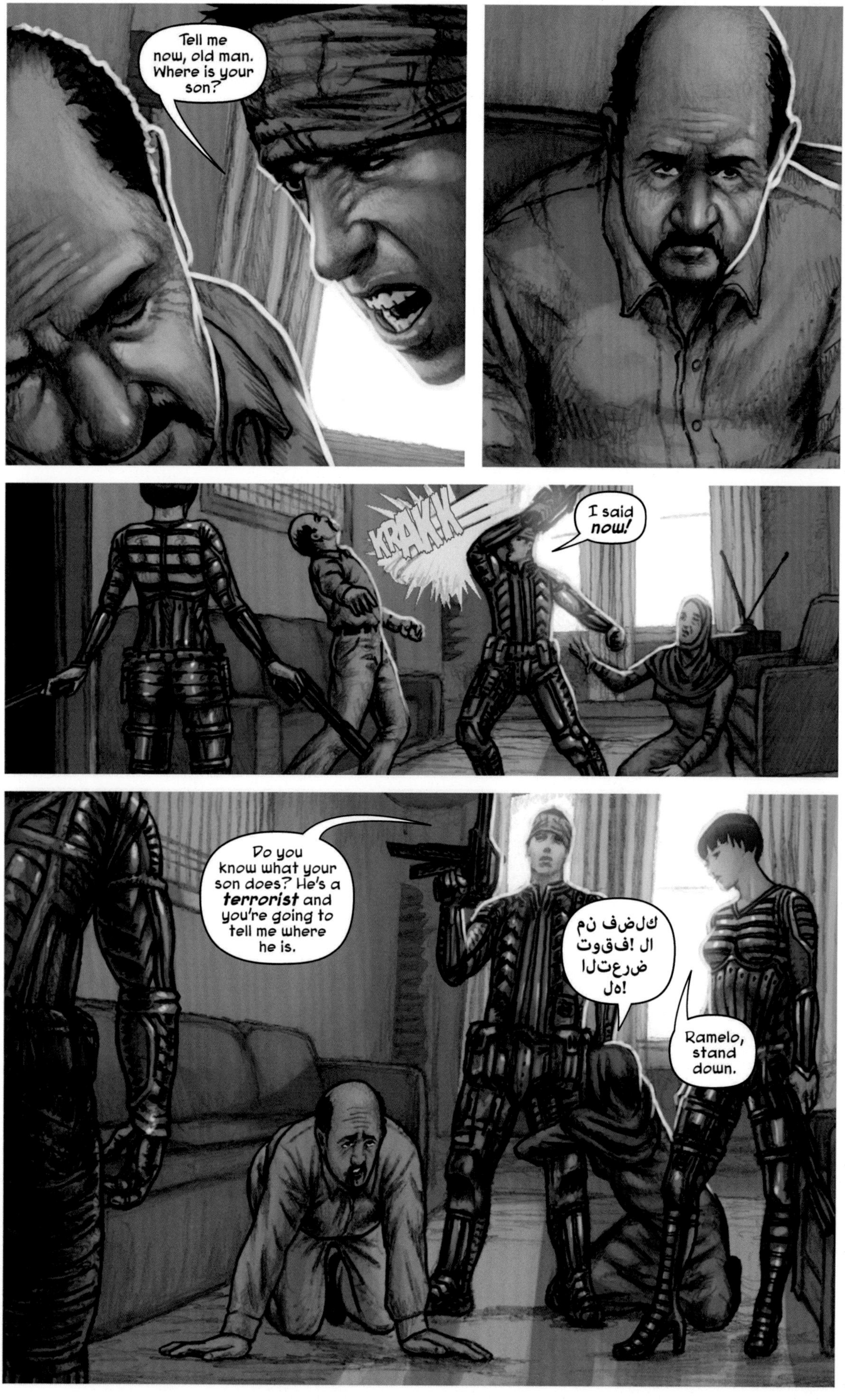
Tell me now, old man. Where is your son?
KRAK-K
I said now!
Do you know what your son does? He's a terrorist and you're going to tell me where he is.
كلضف نم
ال !فقوت
ضرعتلا
!هل
Ramelo, stand down.

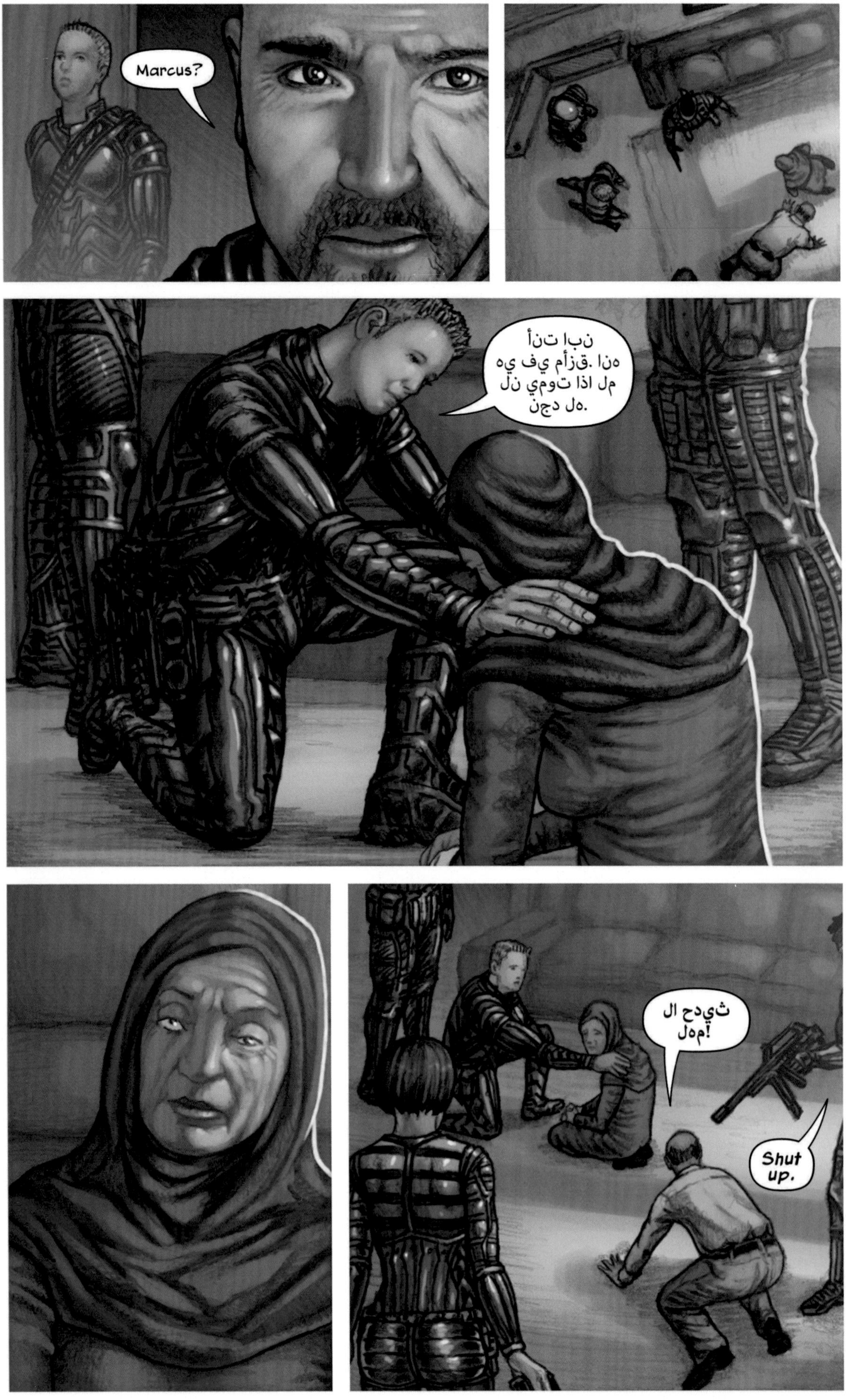
Marcus?
أنت ابن هي في مأزق. انه لن يموت اذا لم نجد له.
ثيدح ال لهم!
Shut up.

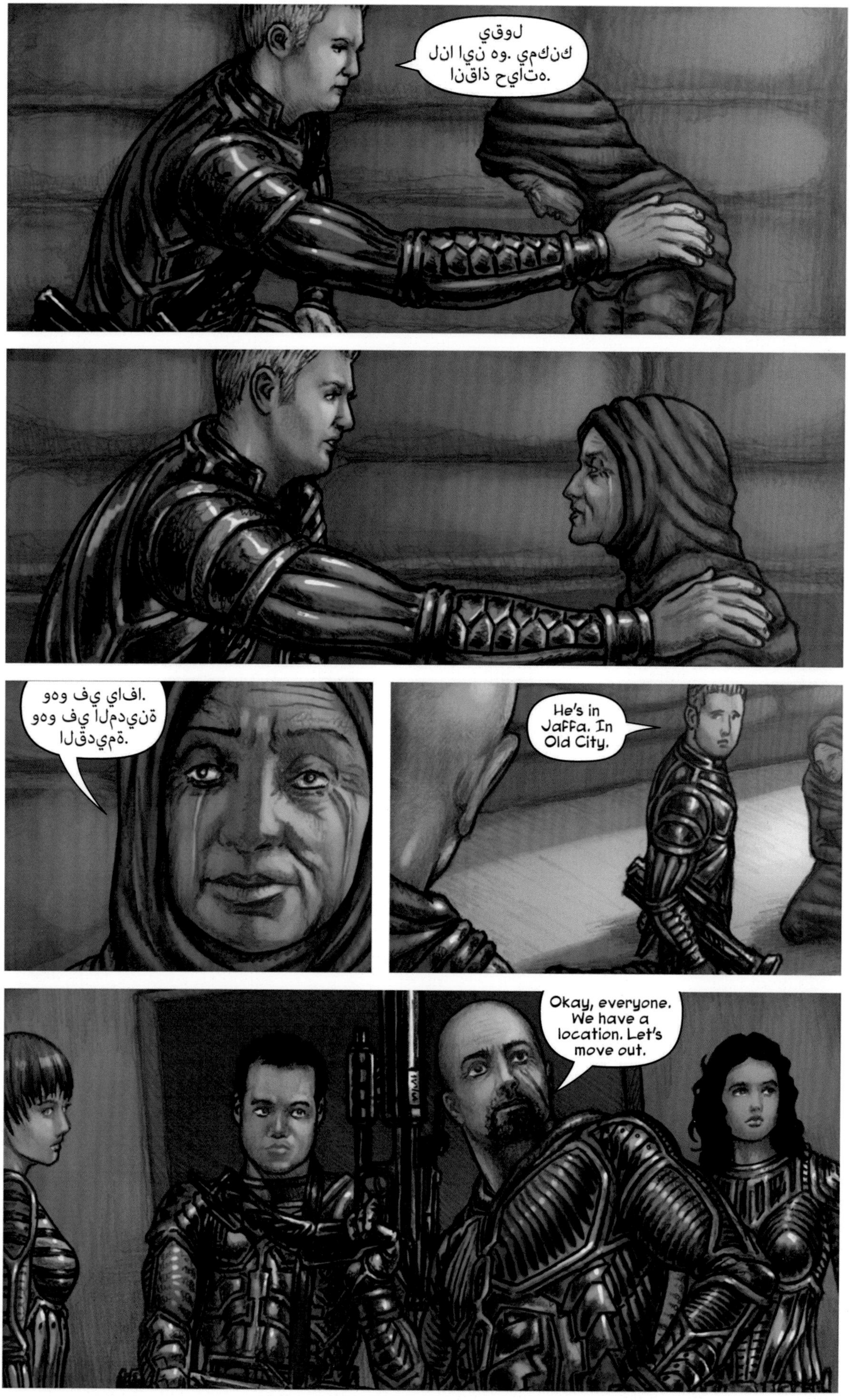
يقول
لنا اين هو. يمكنك
انقاذ حياته.
وهو في يافا.
وهو في المدينة
القديمة.
He's in Jaffa. In Old City.
Okay, everyone. We have a location. Let's move out.

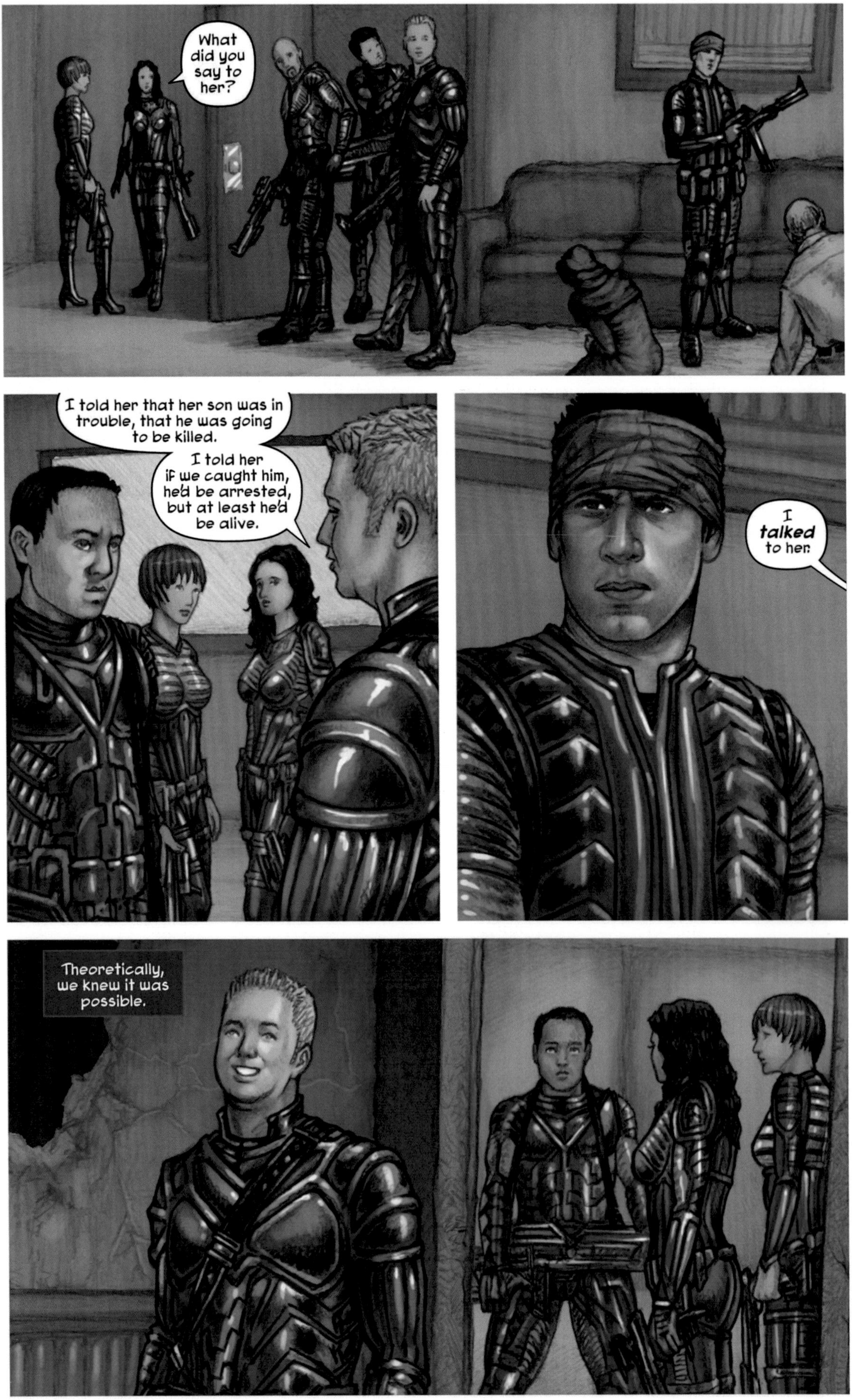
What did you say to her?
I told her that her son was in trouble, that he was going to be killed.
I told her if we caught him, he'd be arrested, but at least he'd be alive.
I *talked* to her.
Theoretically, we knew it was possible.

The numbers worked out.

Pass close enough to a rotating singularity at the right angle with the right velocity...

But nobody really knew what would happen.

Nobody had ever done it.

I have eyes on the subject. He's moving south.

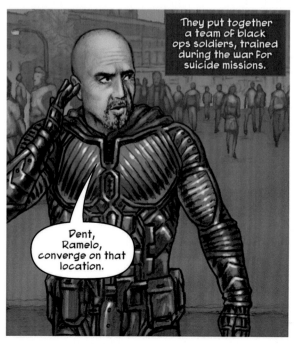

They put together a team of black ops soldiers, trained during the war for suicide missions.

Dent, Ramelo, converge on that location.

That's who you send to the past.

People without any future.

Be careful. There's a hell of a lot of security around here.

Hear that, everyone? Keep your eyes open.

Islie, give me an update on the subject.

He just turned. Heading directly towards you, Ramelo.

We were supposed to get here earlier.

Two weeks before the trigger event, instead of just two days.

Got him. I'm moving in.

Somewhere, something went wrong.

A miscalculation.

Off by a billionth of a decimal point.

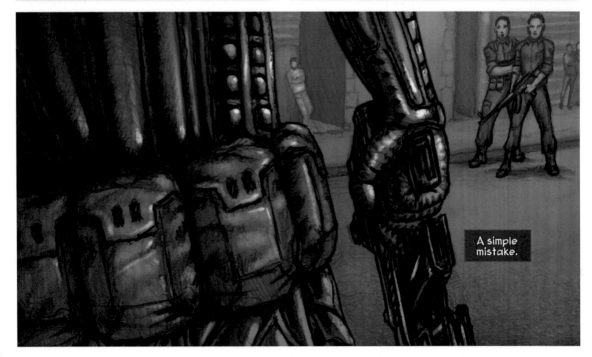

A simple mistake.

BLAM BLAM
BLAM BLAM
BLAM BLAM

BLAM

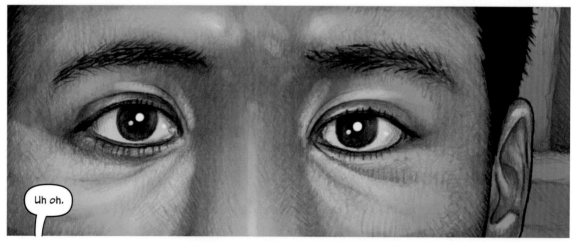

Uh oh.

Subject is on the move! I repeat, subject is on the move!

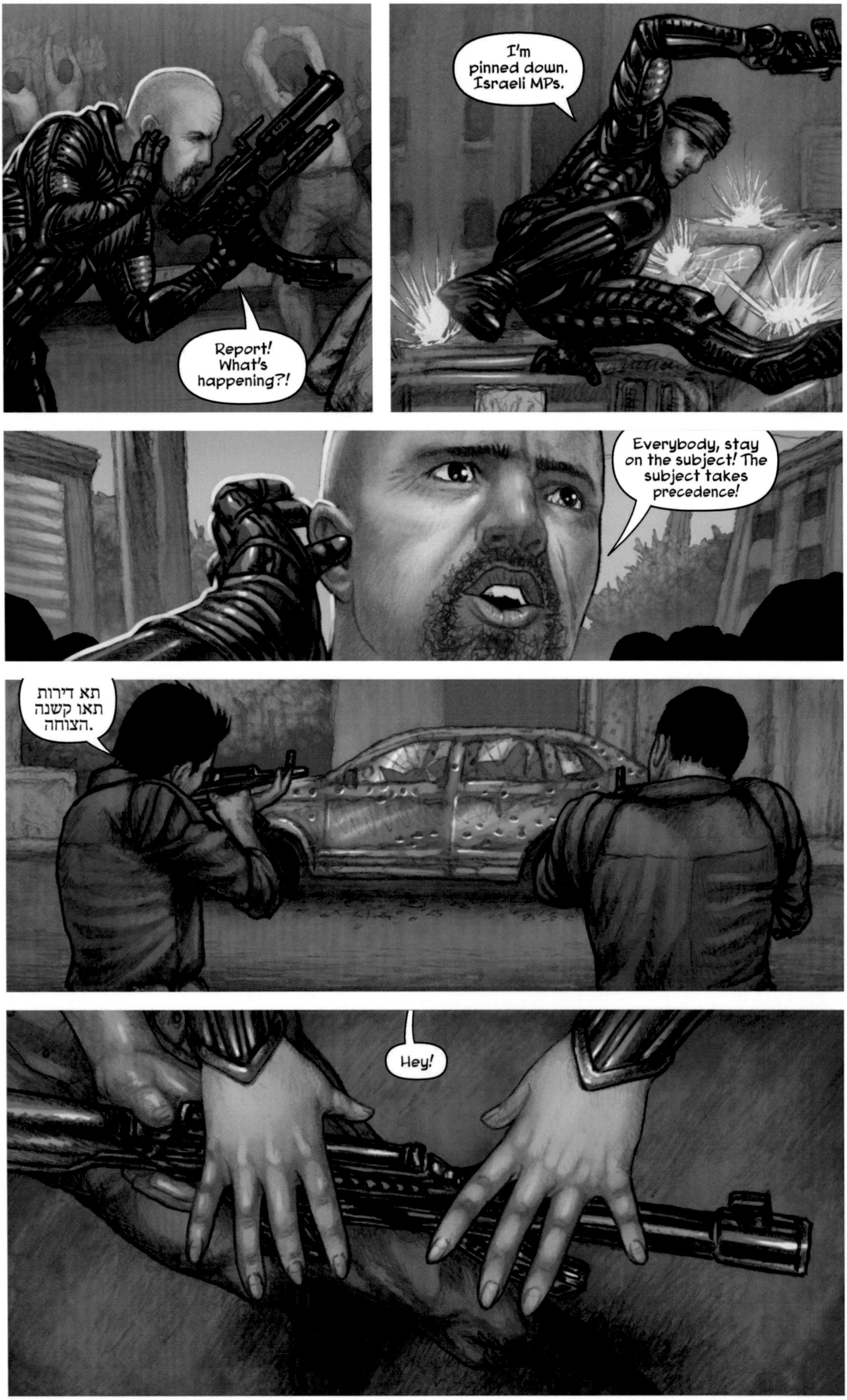
Report! What's happening?!
I'm pinned down. Israeli MPs.
Everybody, stay on the subject! The subject takes precedence!
תא דירות תאו קשנה הצוחה.
Hey!

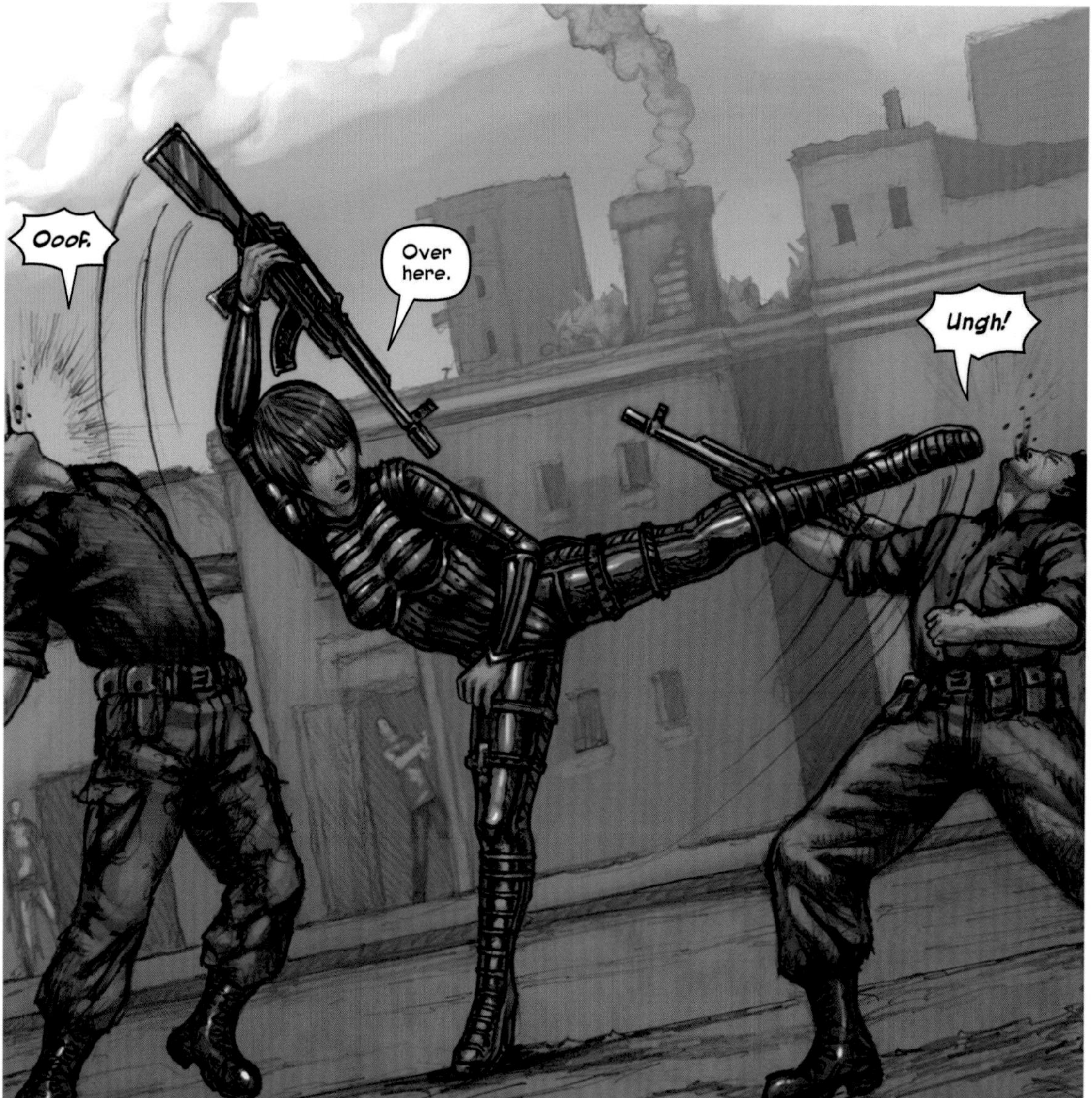
Ooof.
Over here.
Ungh!

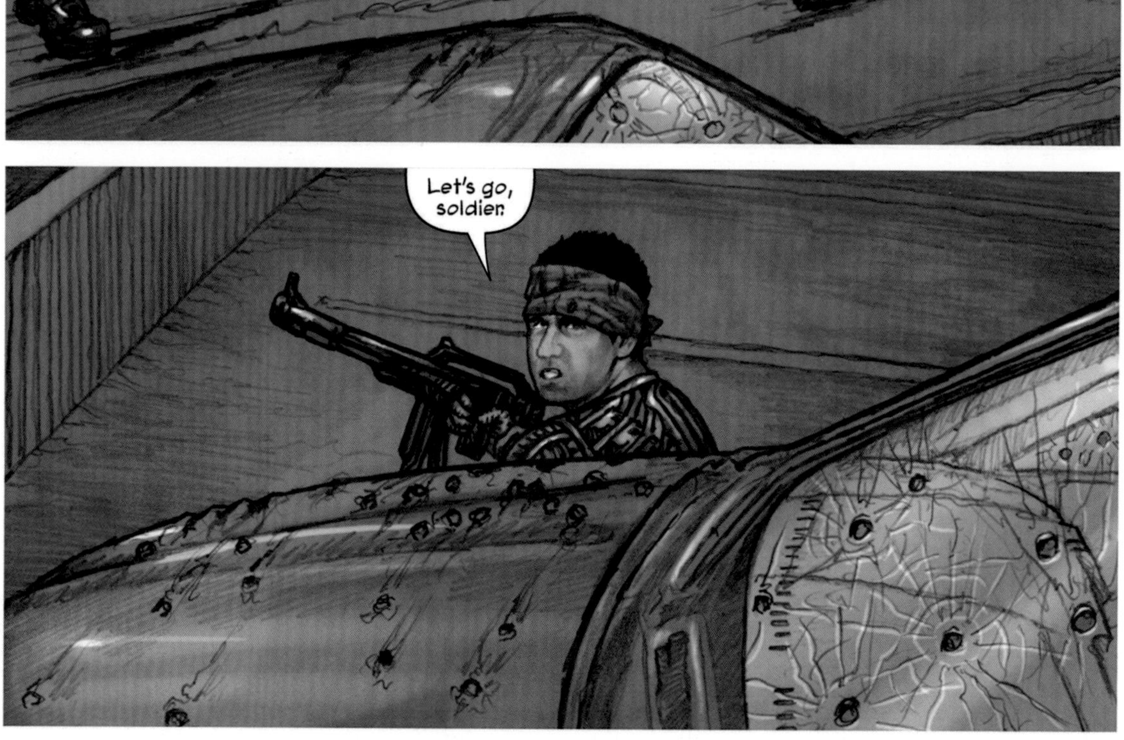
Let's go, soldier.

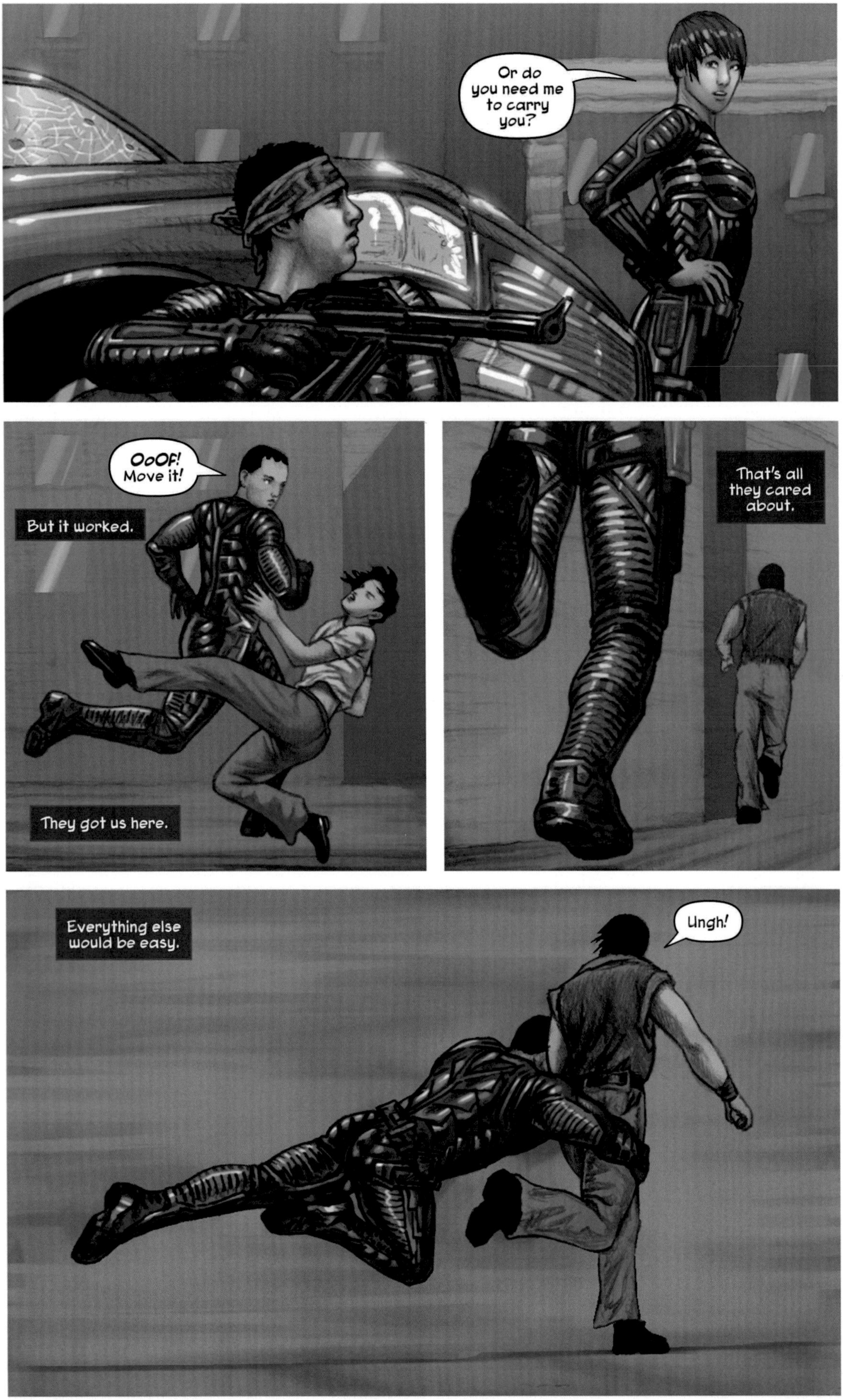
Or do you need me to carry you?
OoOF! Move it!
But it worked.
They got us here.
That's all they cared about.
Everything else would be easy.
Ungh!

GOTCHA!

Capture the assassin, make him lead us to the other conspirators.

Beat it out of him, if we had to.

Do you have any idea what you did? Do you?!

Of course it would work.

After all, we had the greatest advantage possible.

Do you have any...

We knew what was coming next.

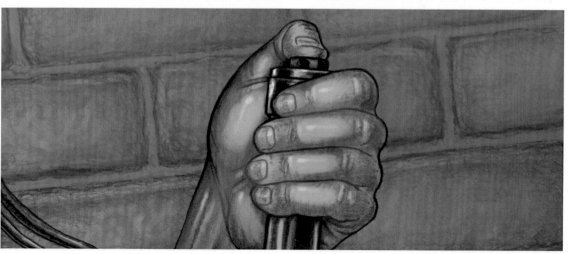

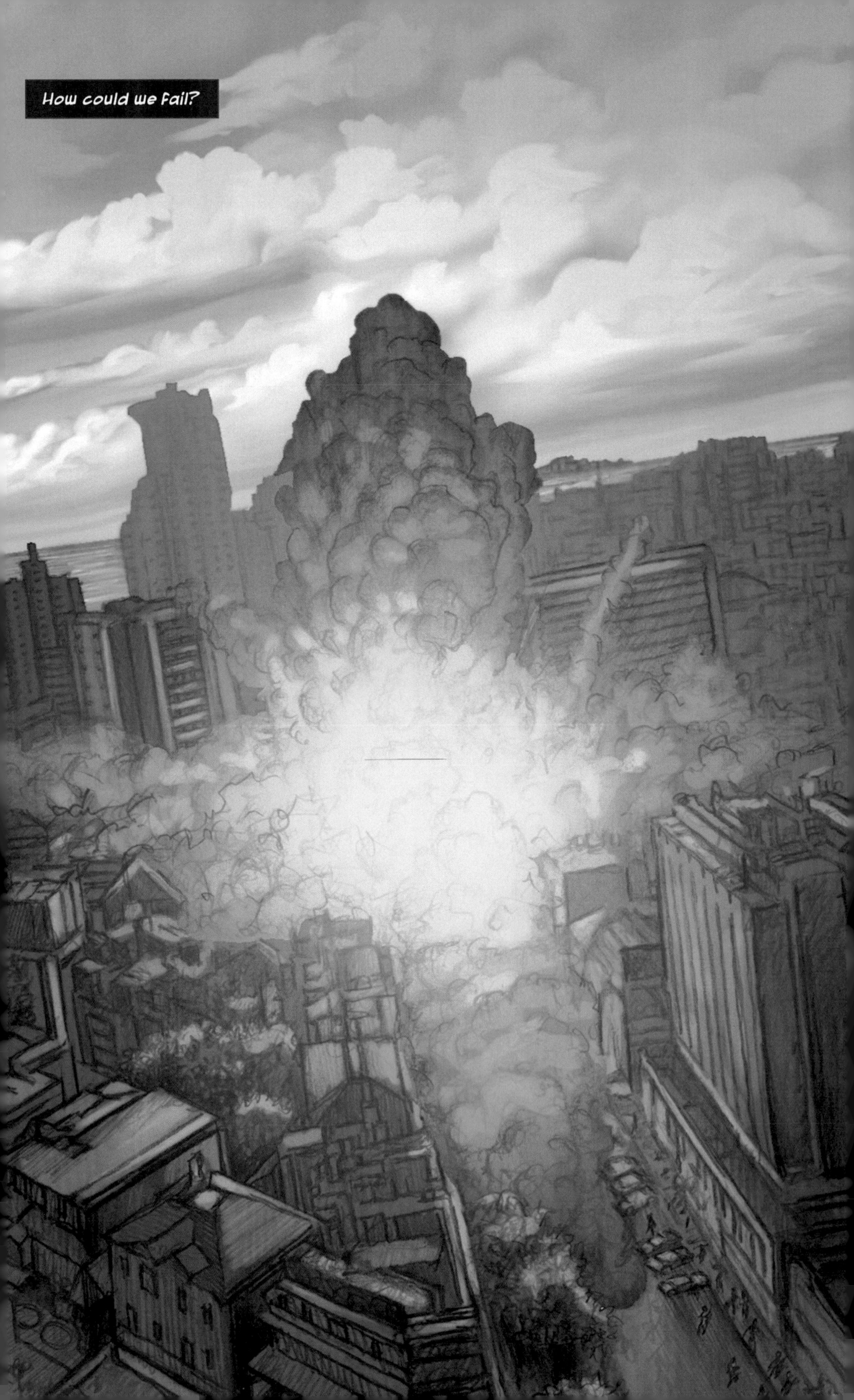
How could we fail?

Chapter Two

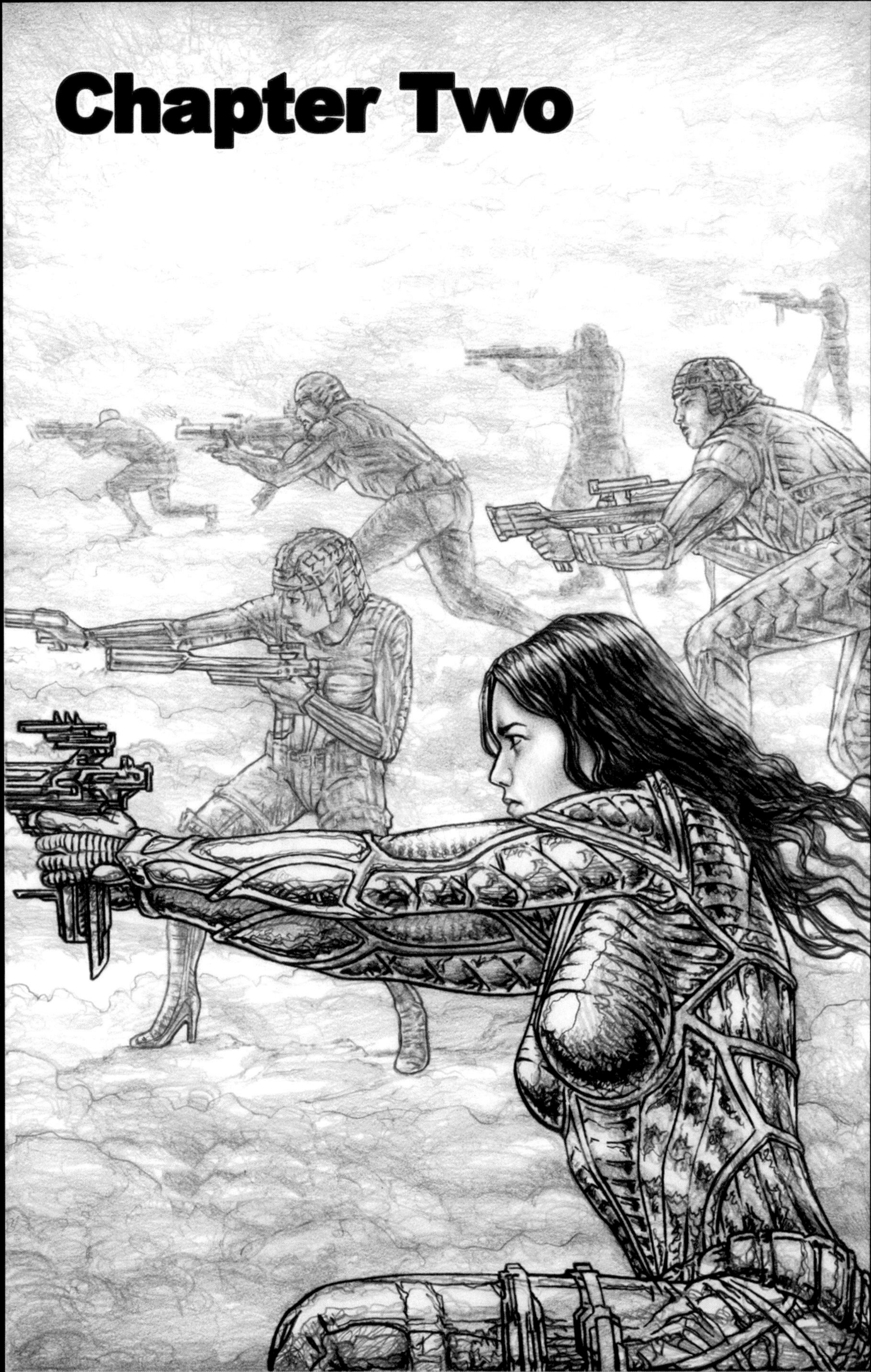

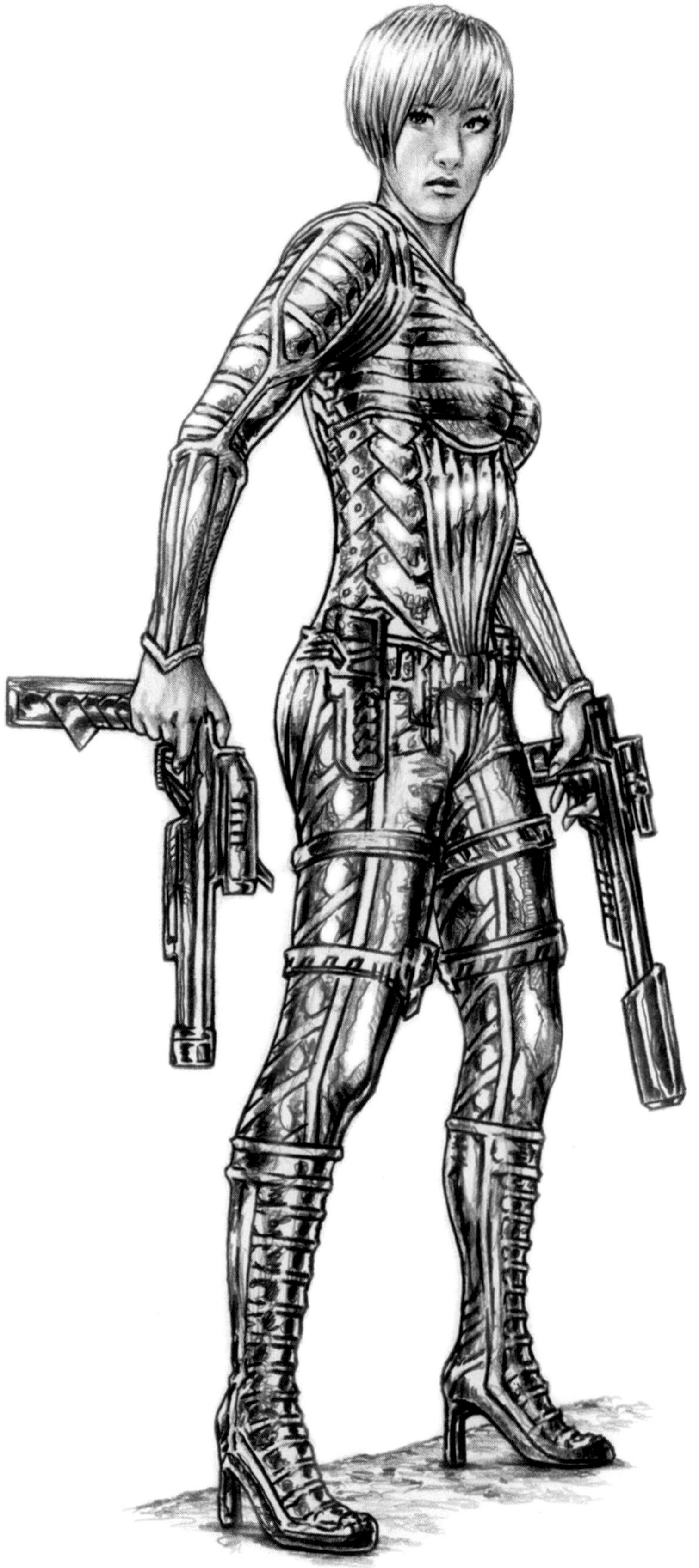

"ISLIE"

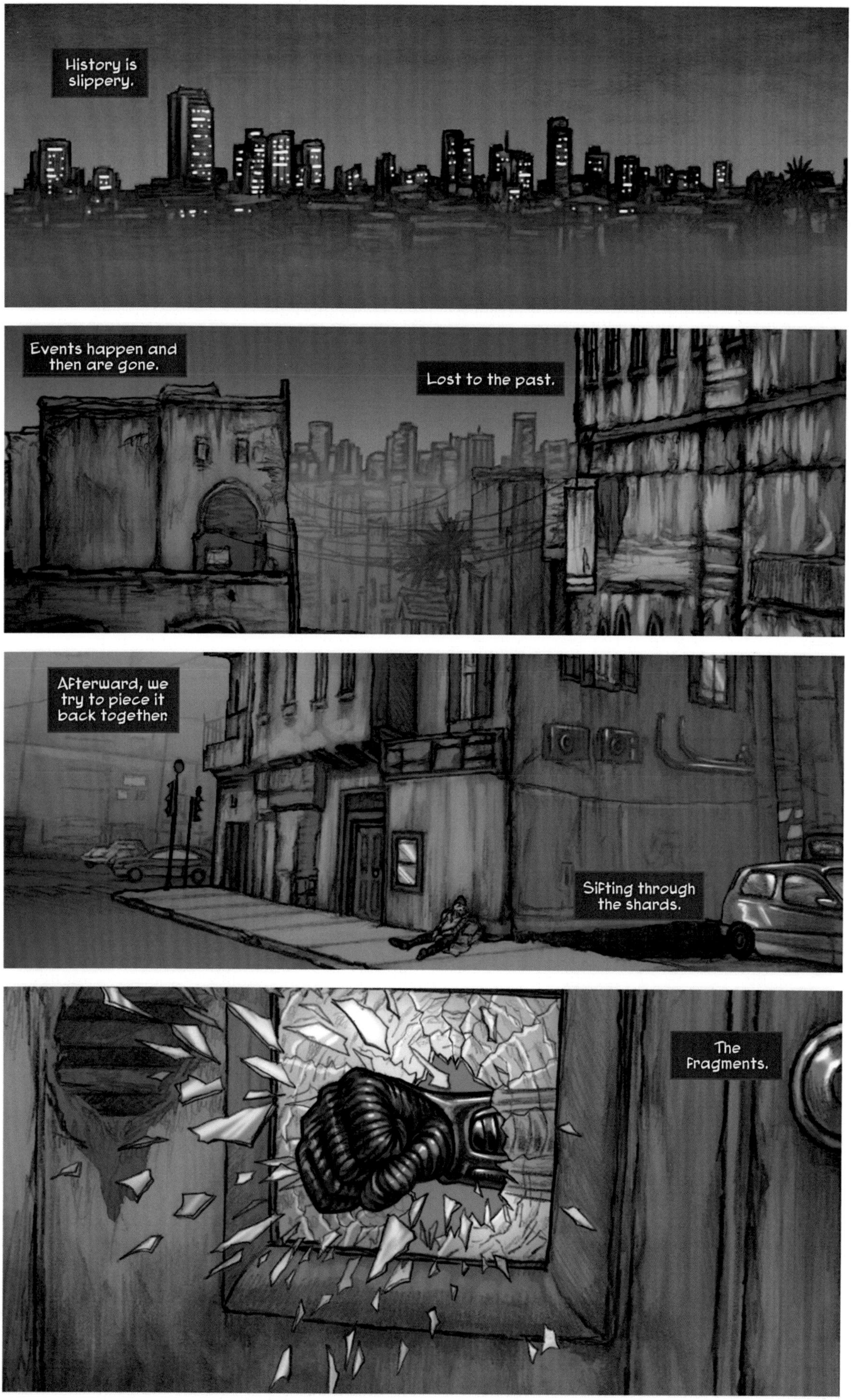
History is slippery.
Events happen and then are gone.
Lost to the past.
Afterward, we try to piece it back together.
Sifting through the shards.
The fragments.

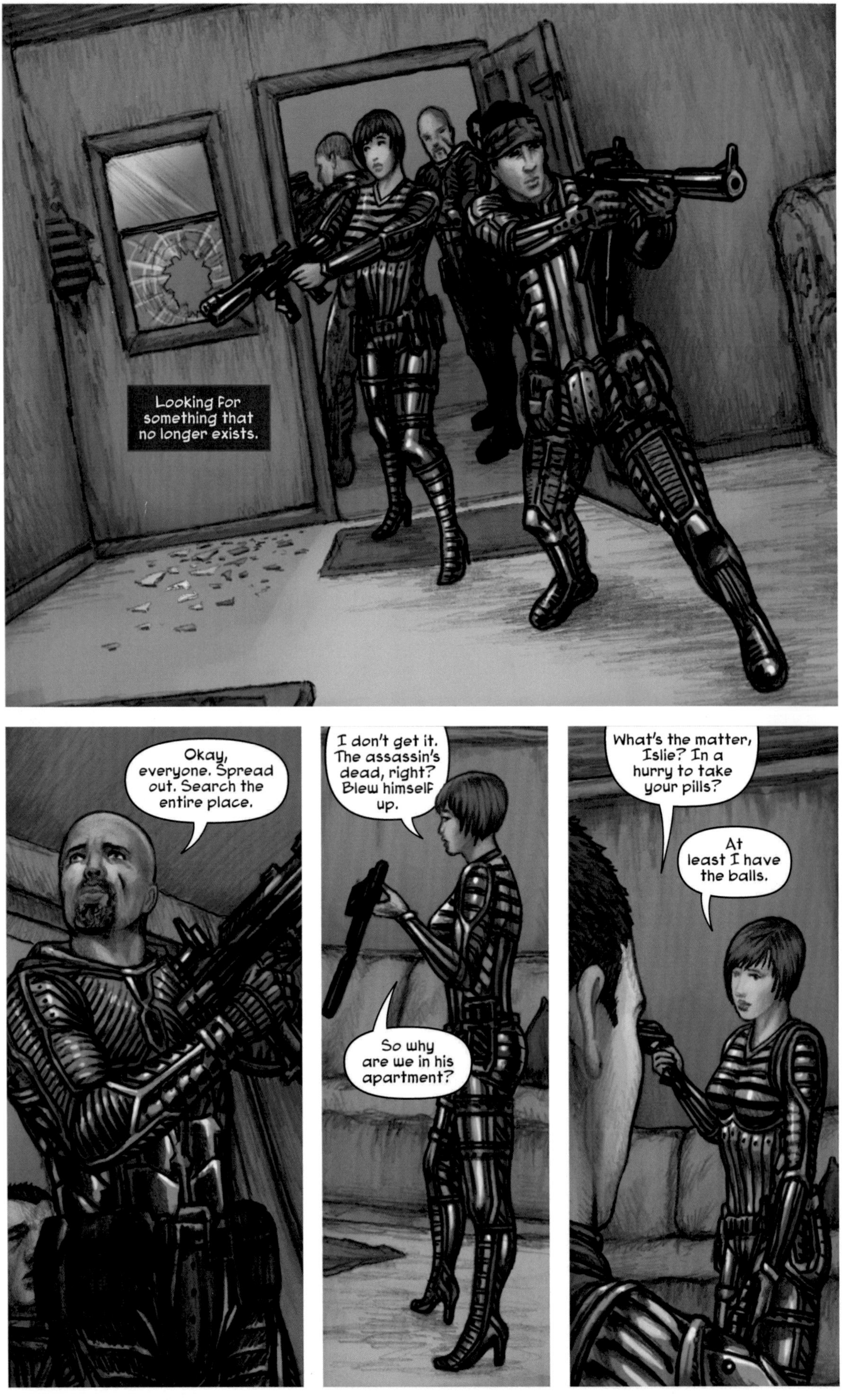
Looking for something that no longer exists.
Okay, everyone. Spread out. Search the entire place.
I don't get it. The assassin's dead, right? Blew himself up.
So why are we in his apartment?
What's the matter, Islie? In a hurry to take your pills?
At least I have the balls.

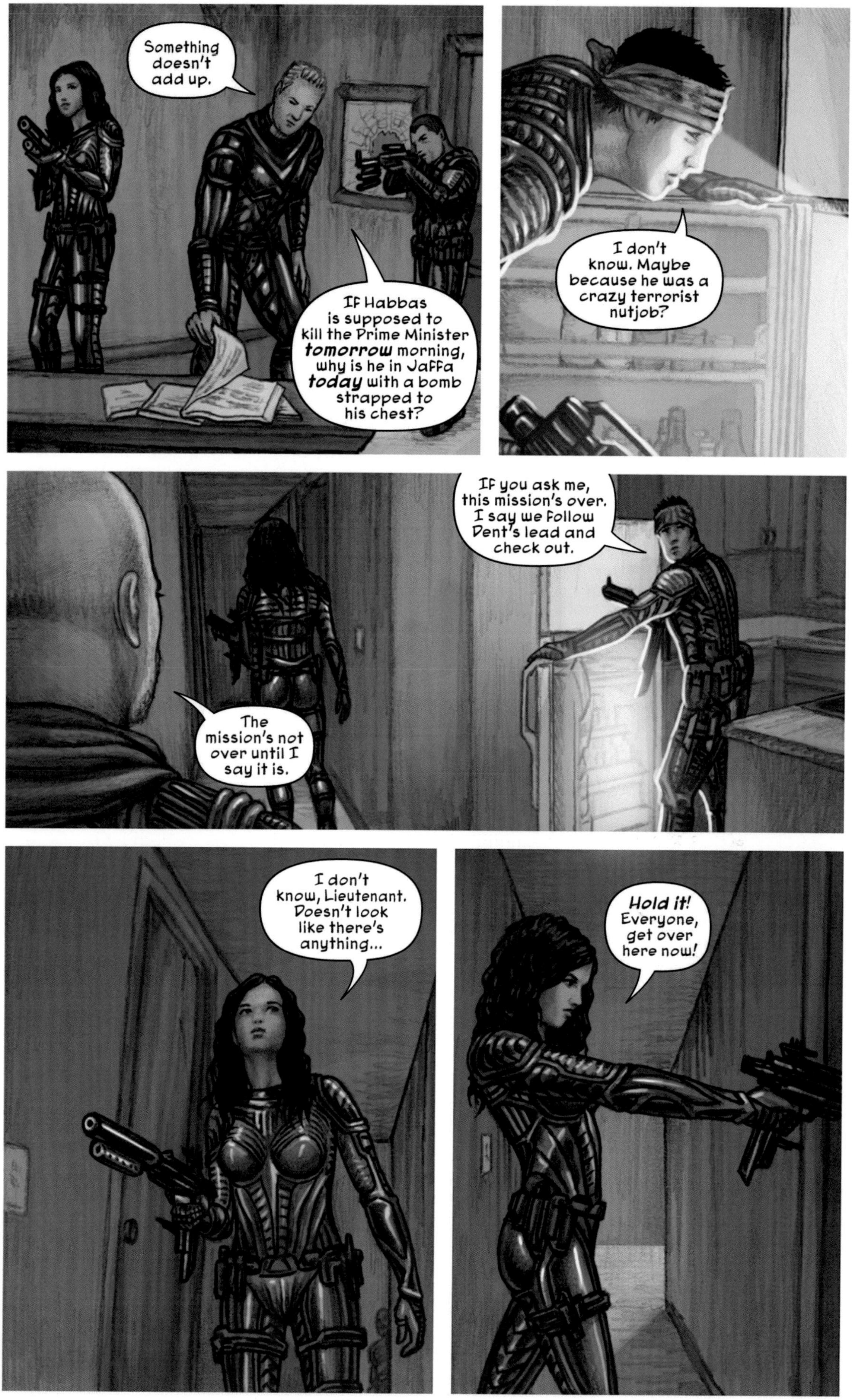
Something doesn't add up.
If Habbas is supposed to kill the Prime Minister *tomorrow* morning, why is he in Jaffa *today* with a bomb strapped to his chest?
I don't know. Maybe because he was a crazy terrorist nutjob?
If you ask me, this mission's over. I say we follow Dent's lead and check out.
The mission's not over until I say it is.
I don't know, Lieutenant. Doesn't look like there's anything...
Hold it! Everyone, get over here now!

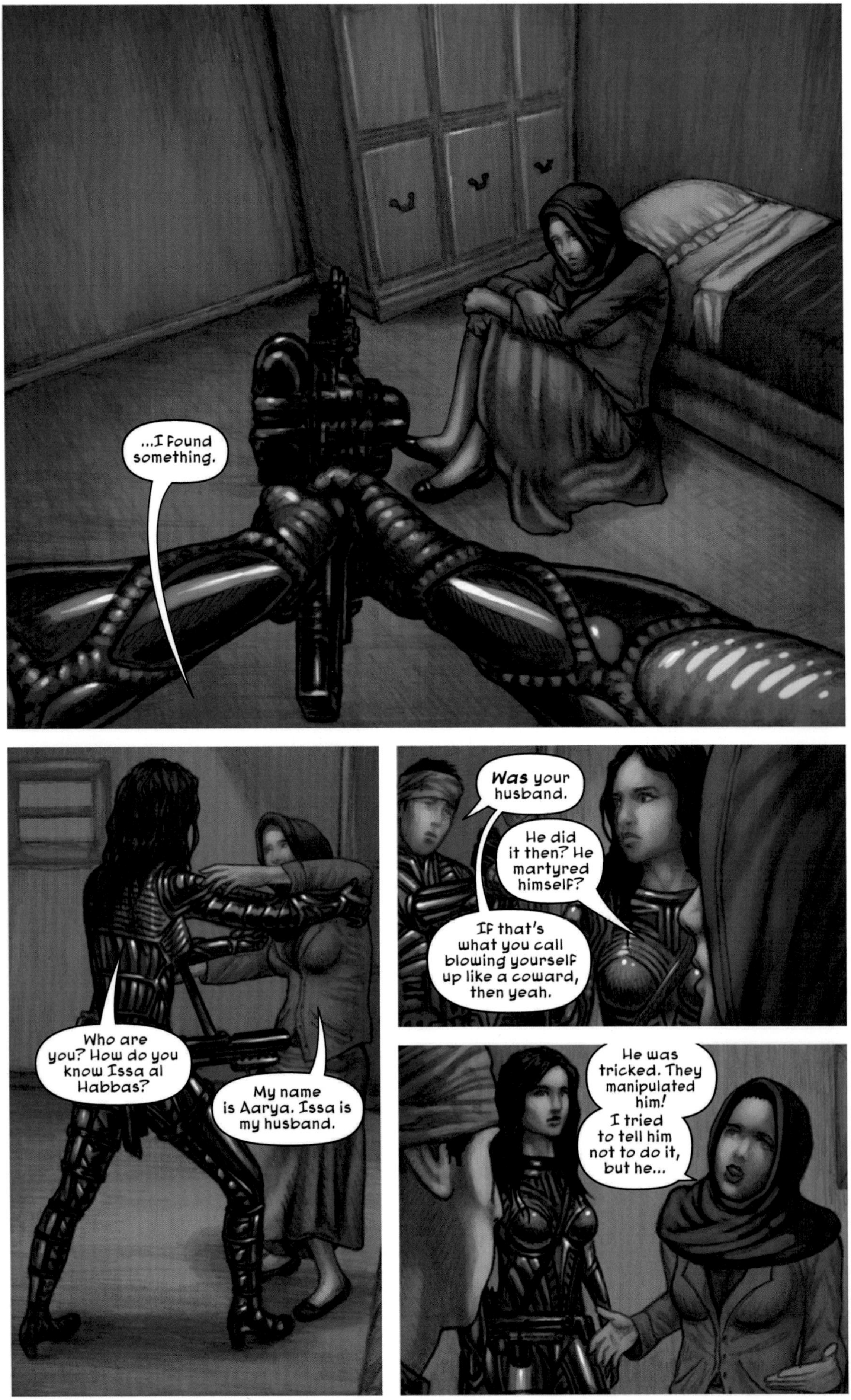
...I found something.
Who are you? How do you know Issa al Habbas?
My name is Aarya. Issa is my husband.
Was your husband.
He did it then? He martyred himself?
If that's what you call blowing yourself up like a coward, then yeah.
He was tricked. They manipulated him!
I tried to tell him not to do it, but he...

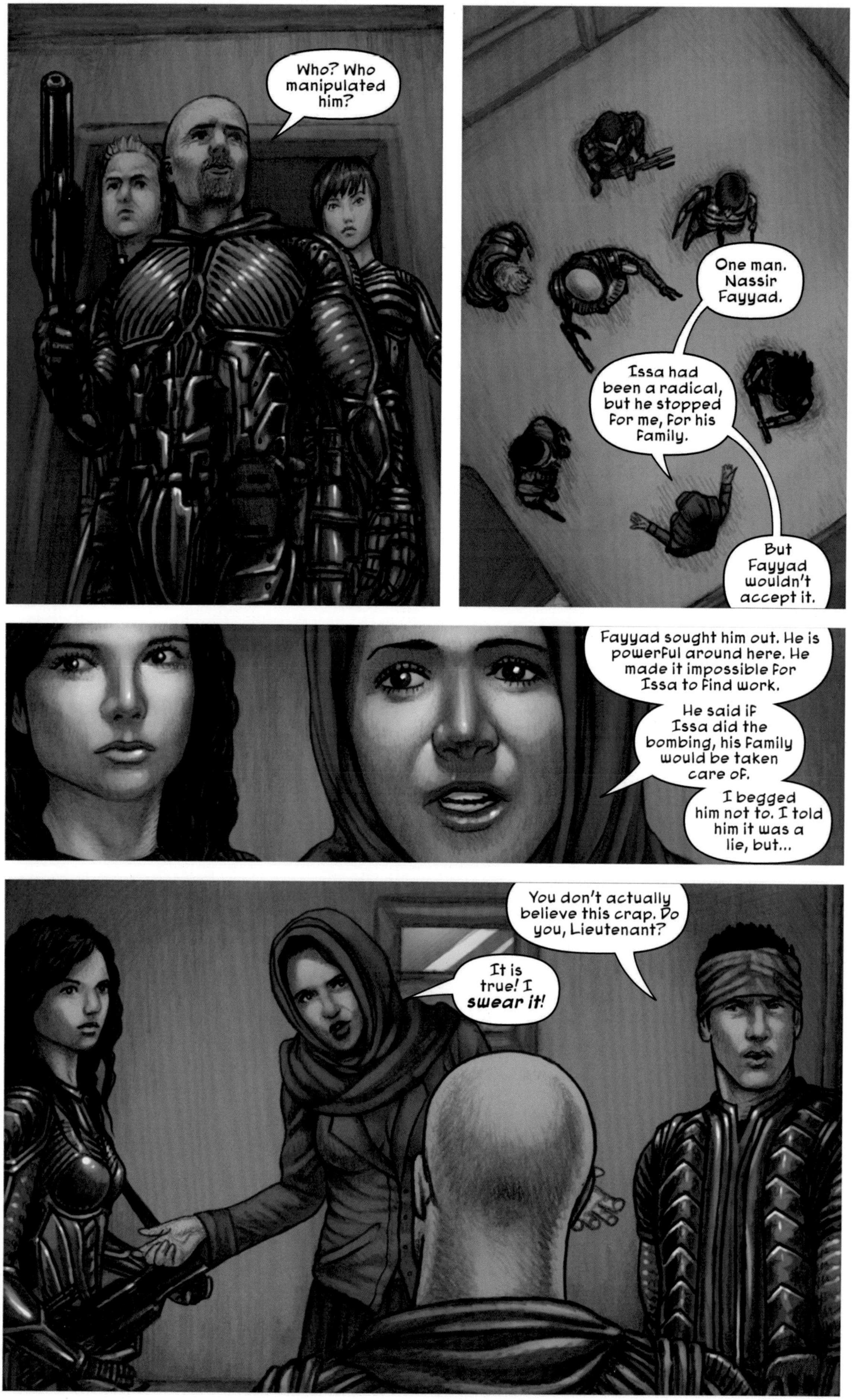
Who? Who manipulated him?
One man. Nassir Fayyad.
Issa had been a radical, but he stopped for me, for his family.
But Fayyad wouldn't accept it.
Fayyad sought him out. He is powerful around here. He made it impossible for Issa to find work.
He said if Issa did the bombing, his family would be taken care of.
I begged him not to. I told him it was a lie, but...
You don't actually believe this crap. Do you, Lieutenant?
It is true! I *swear it!*

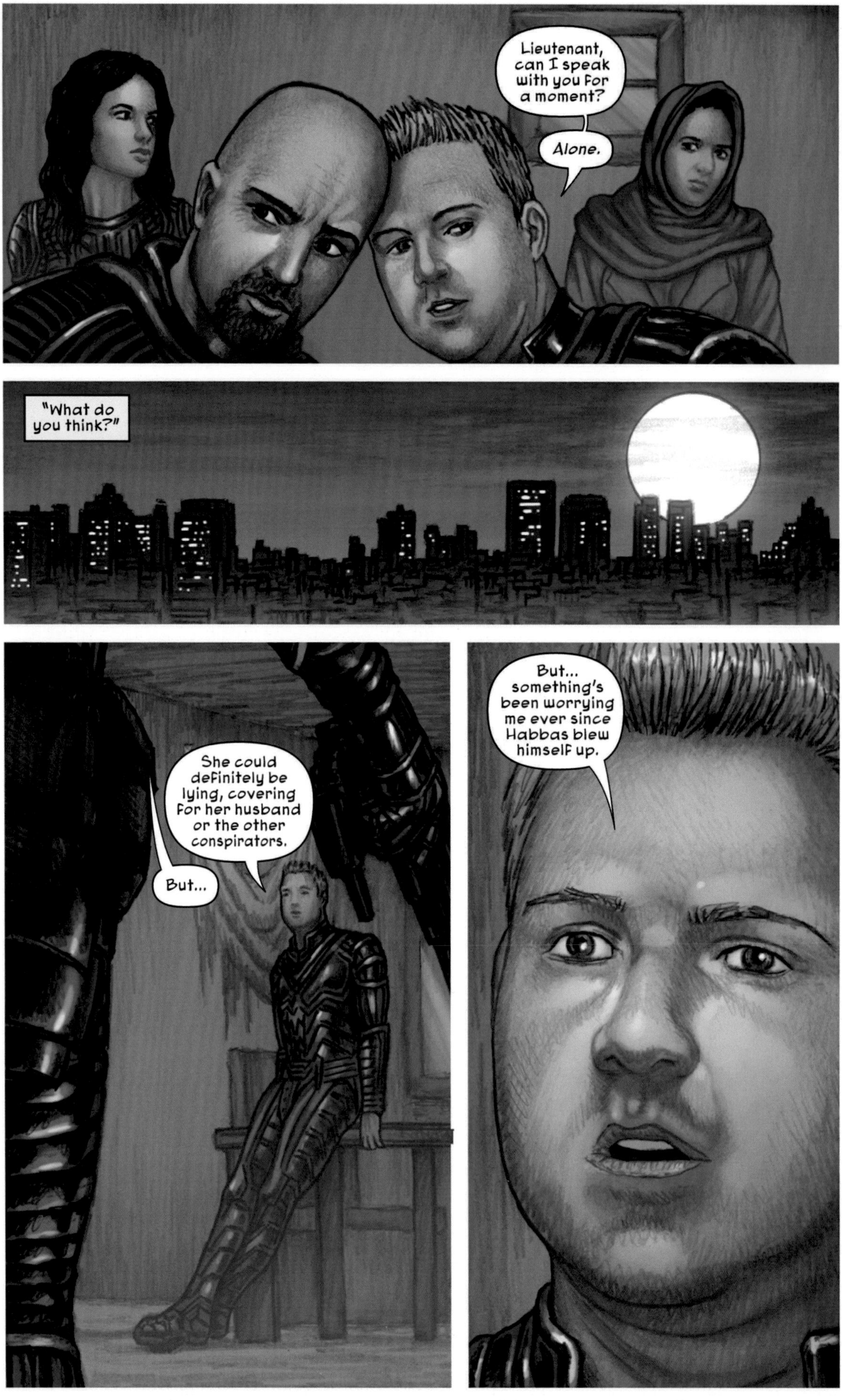
Lieutenant, can I speak with you for a moment?
Alone.
"What do you think?"
She could definitely be lying, covering for her husband or the other conspirators.
But...
But... something's been worrying me ever since Habbas blew himself up.

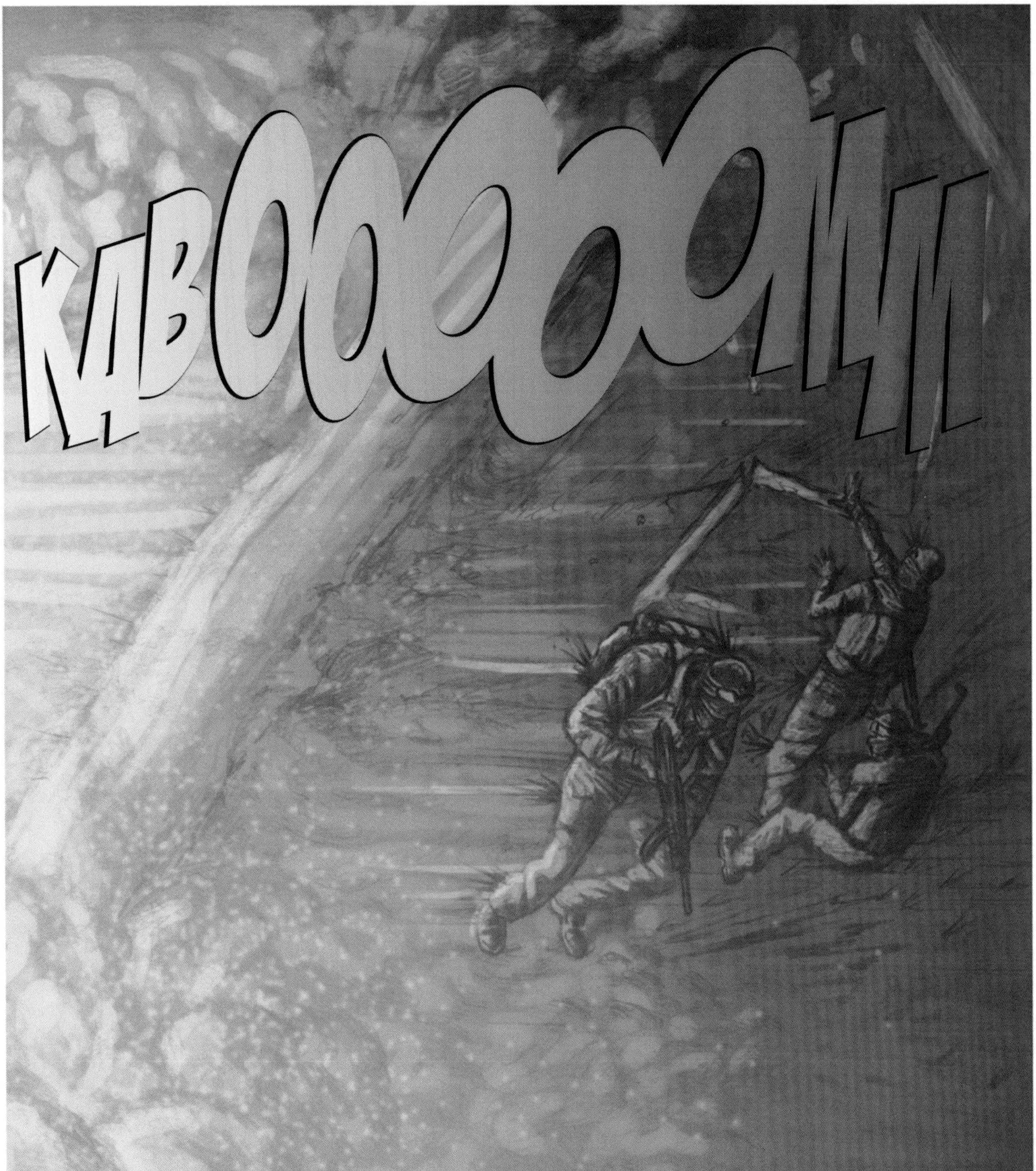
KABOOOOOM

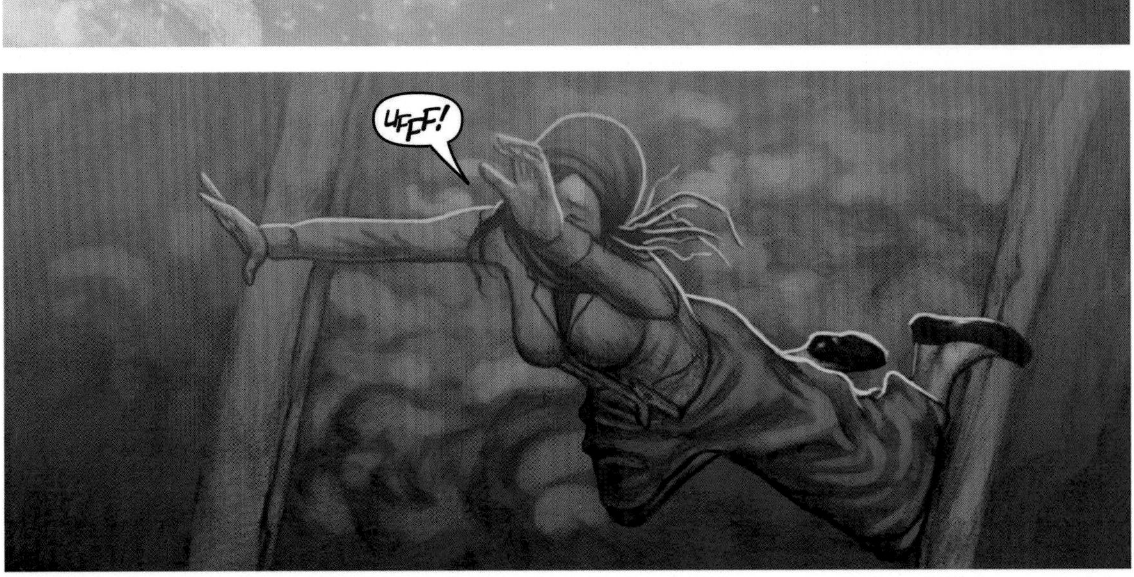
UFFF!

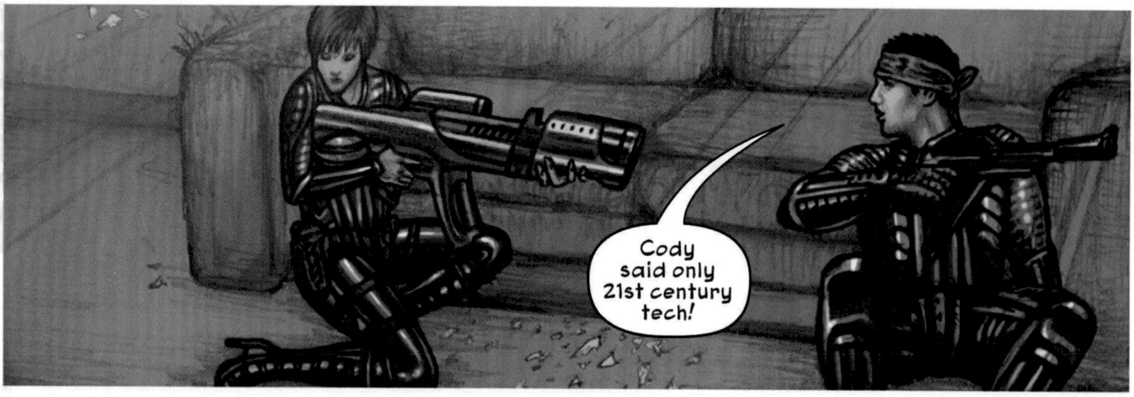
Cody said only 21st century tech!

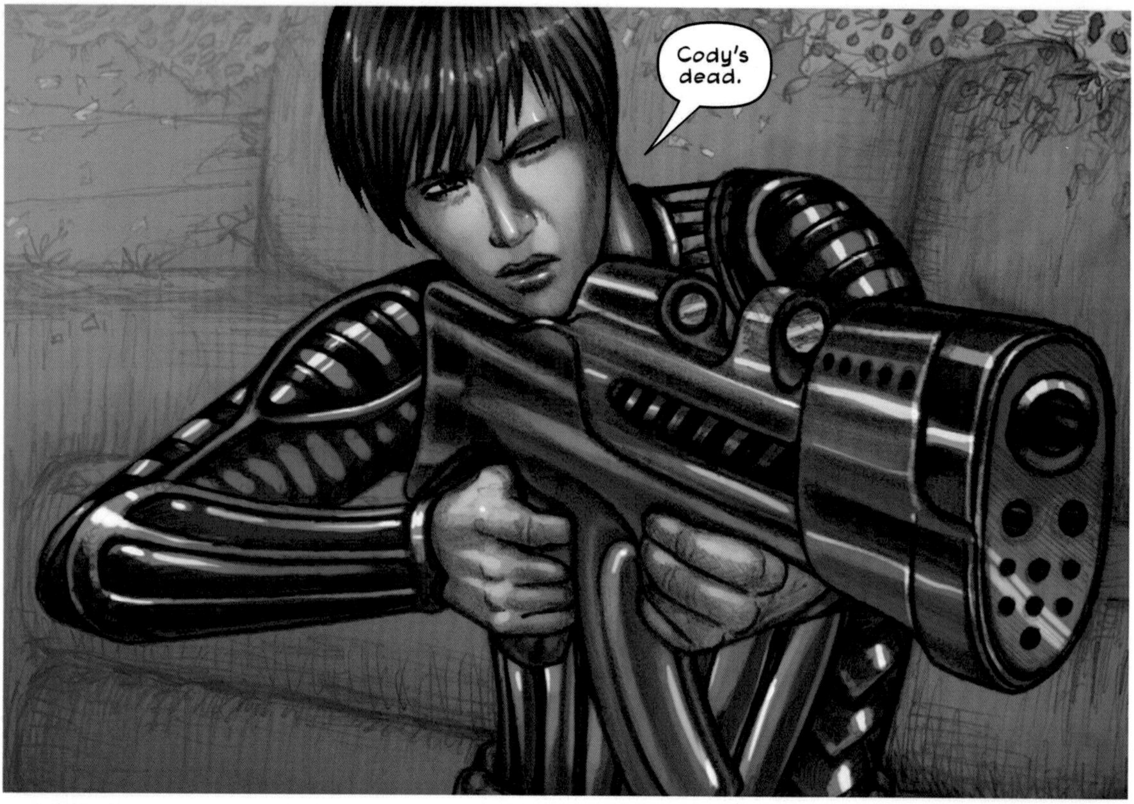
Cody's dead.

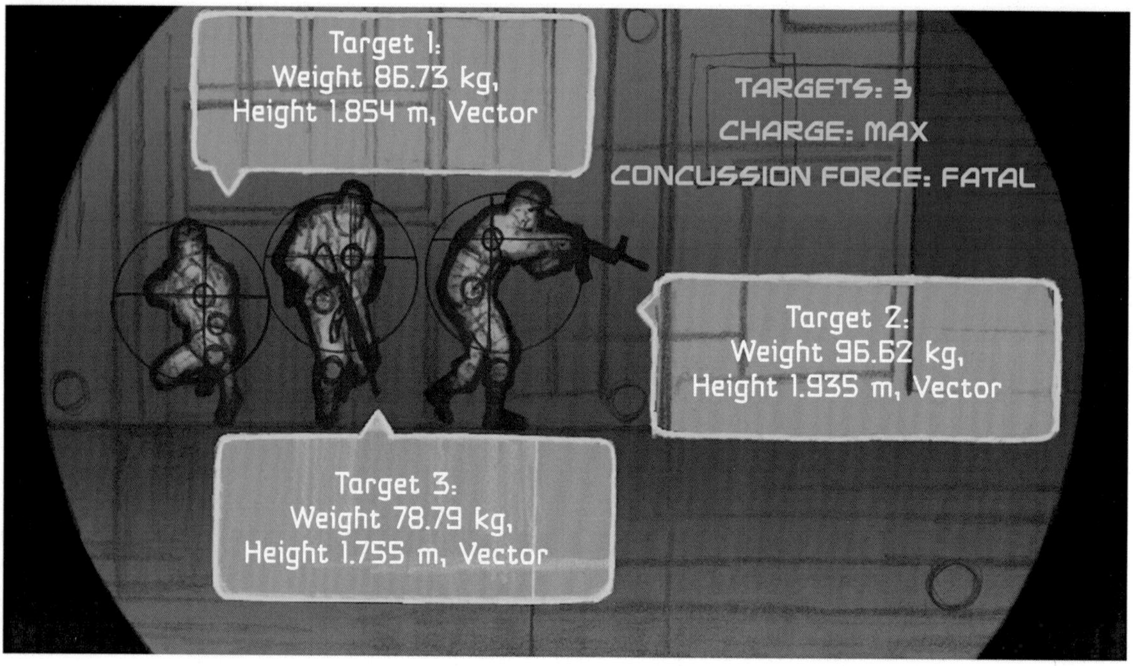
Target 1:
Weight 86.73 kg,
Height 1.854 m, Vector
TARGETS: 3
CHARGE: MAX
CONCUSSION FORCE: FATAL
Target 2:
Weight 96.62 kg,
Height 1.935 m, Vector
Target 3:
Weight 78.79 kg,
Height 1.755 m, Vector

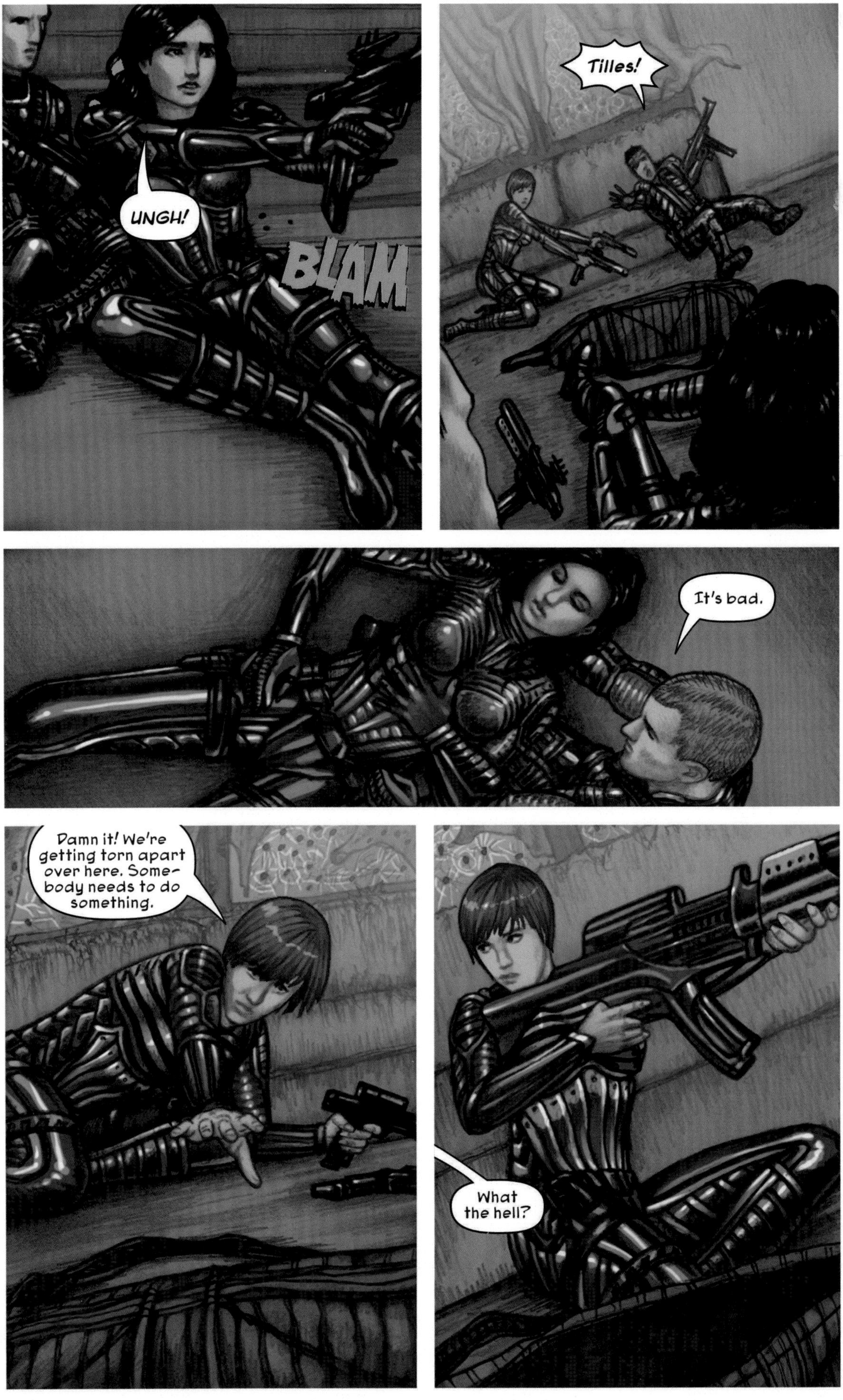
UNGH!
BLAM
Tilles!
It's bad.
Damn it! We're getting torn apart over here. Somebody needs to do something.
What the hell?

They are coming to kill us. We have to get out of here!

Aarya! No, wait! Stay here!

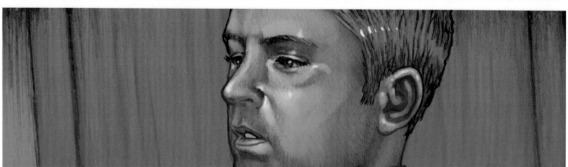

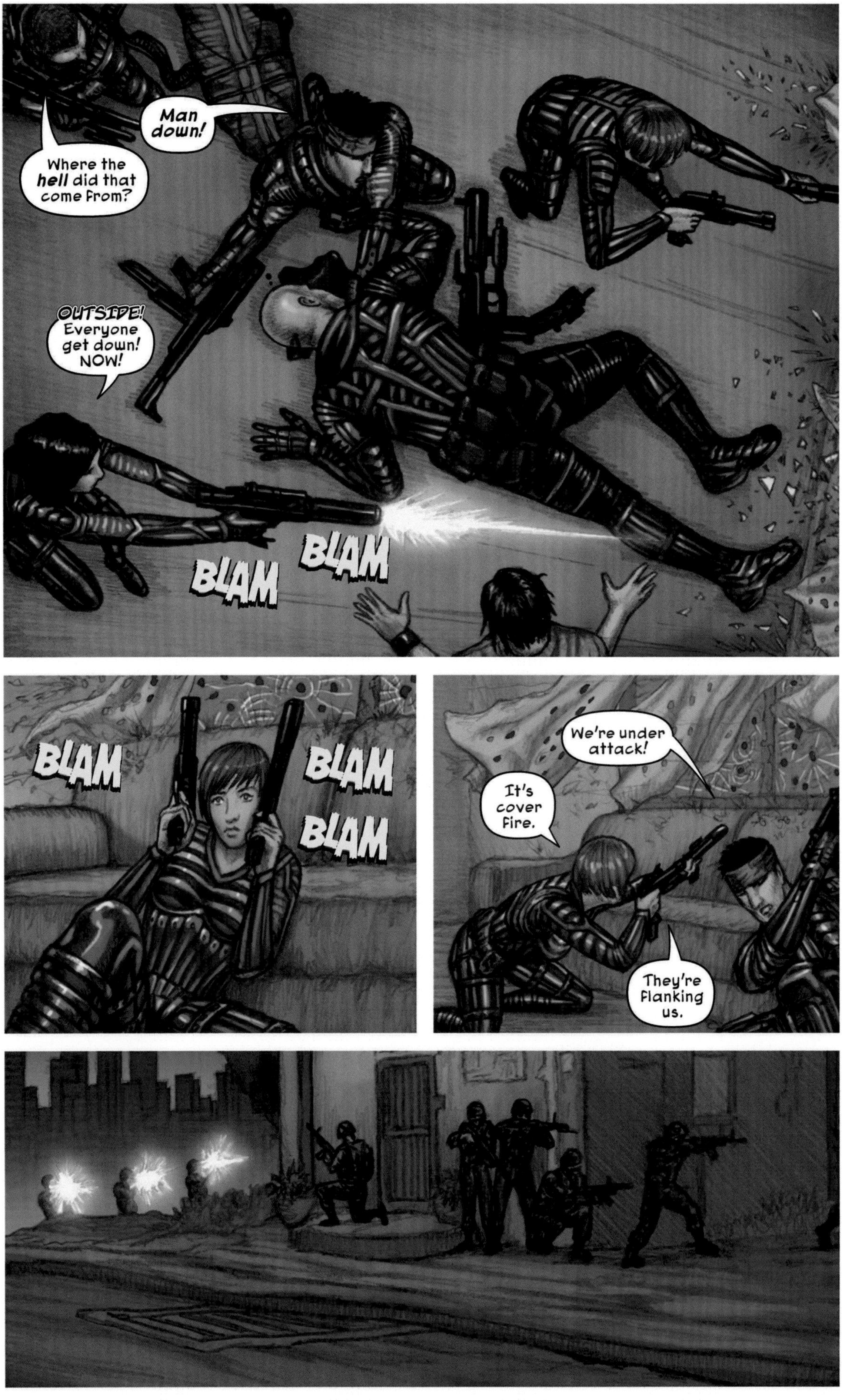
Where the *hell* did that come from?
Man down!
OUTSIDE! Everyone get down! NOW!
BLAM
BLAM
BLAM
BLAM
BLAM
We're under attack!
It's cover fire.
They're flanking us.

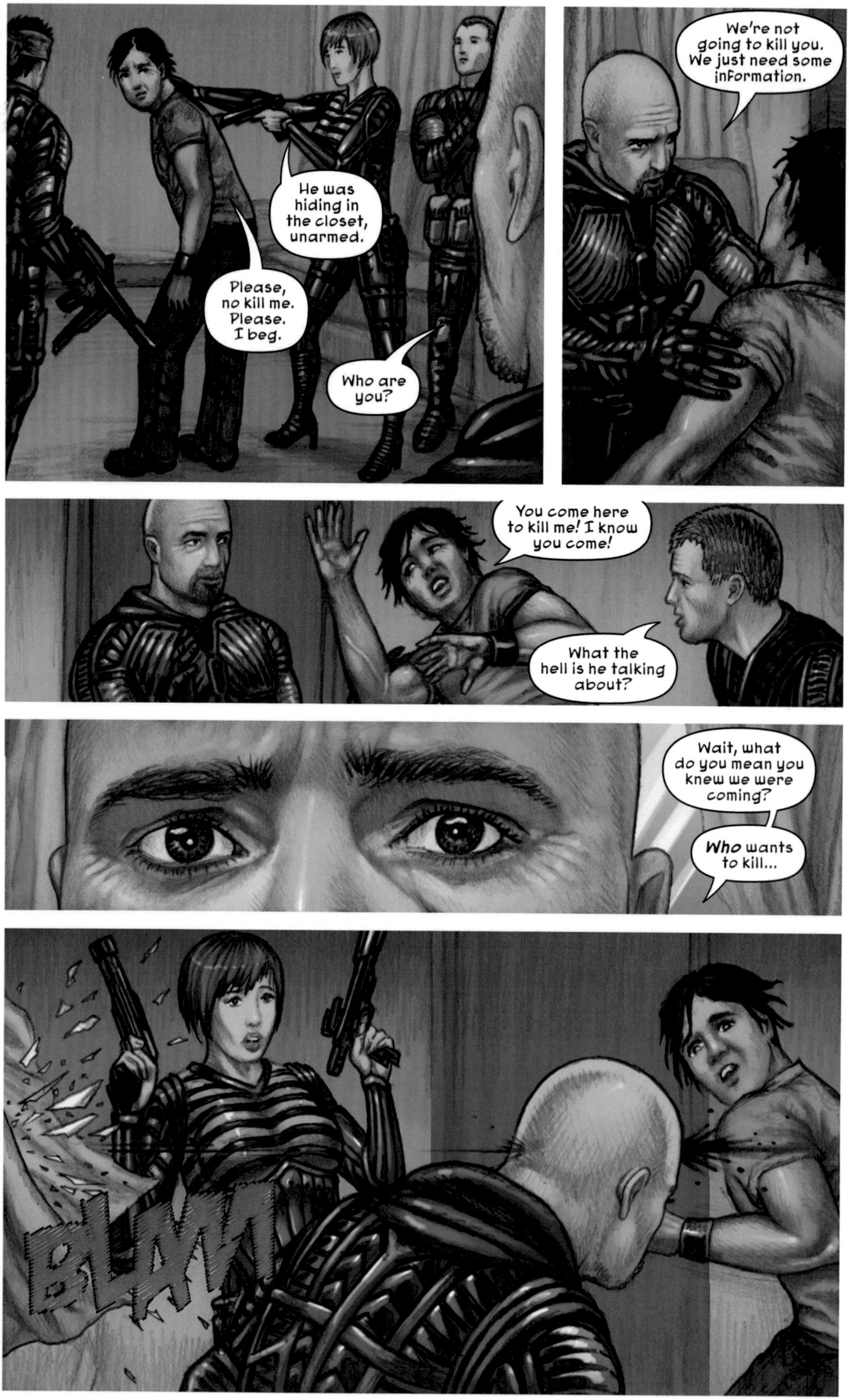
He was hiding in the closet, unarmed.
Please, no kill me. Please. I beg.
Who are you?
We're not going to kill you. We just need some information.
You come here to kill me! I know you come!
What the hell is he talking about?
Wait, what do you mean you knew we were coming?
Who wants to kill...
BLAM!

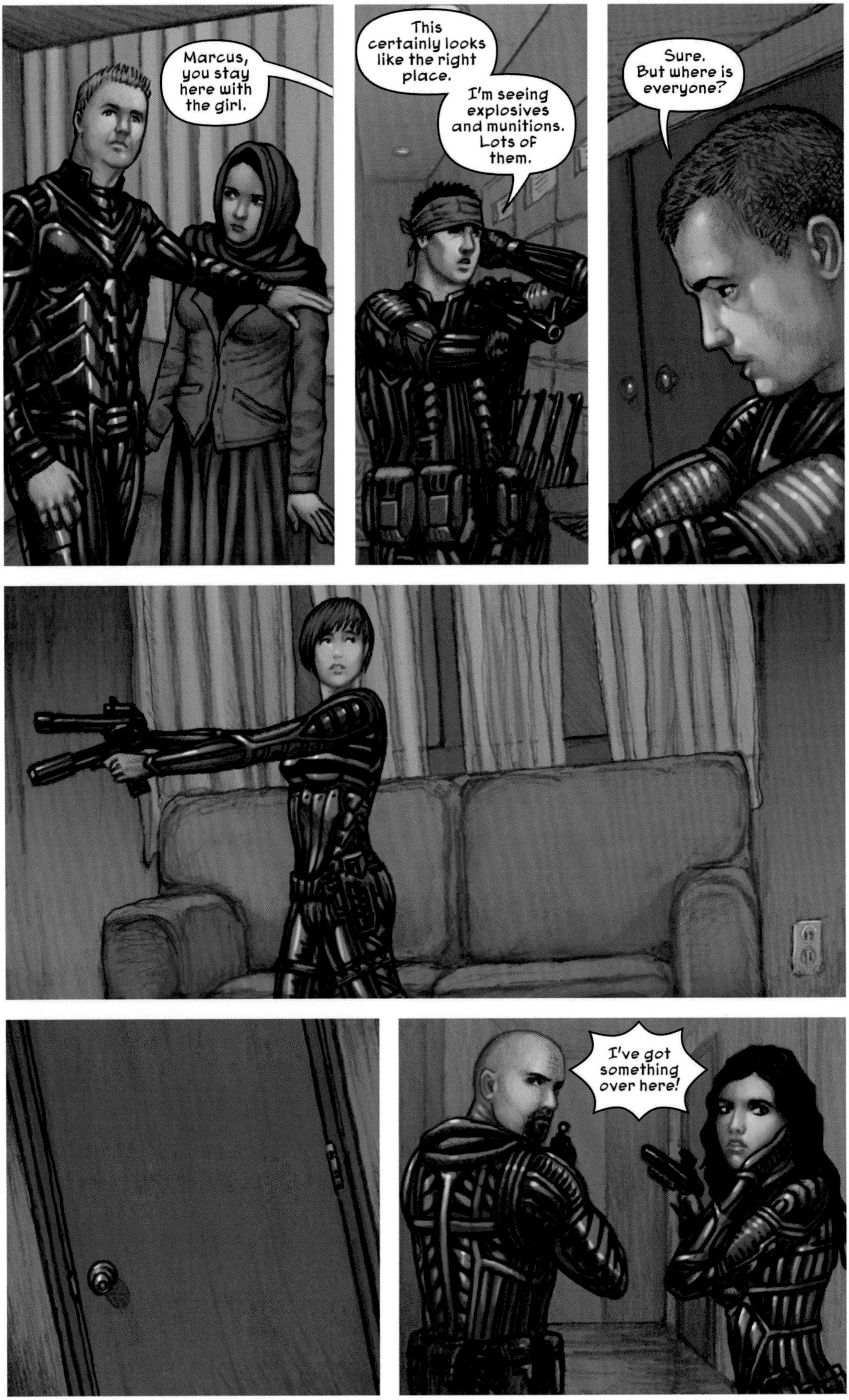
Marcus, you stay here with the girl.
This certainly looks like the right place.
I'm seeing explosives and munitions. Lots of them.
Sure. But where is everyone?
I've got something over here!

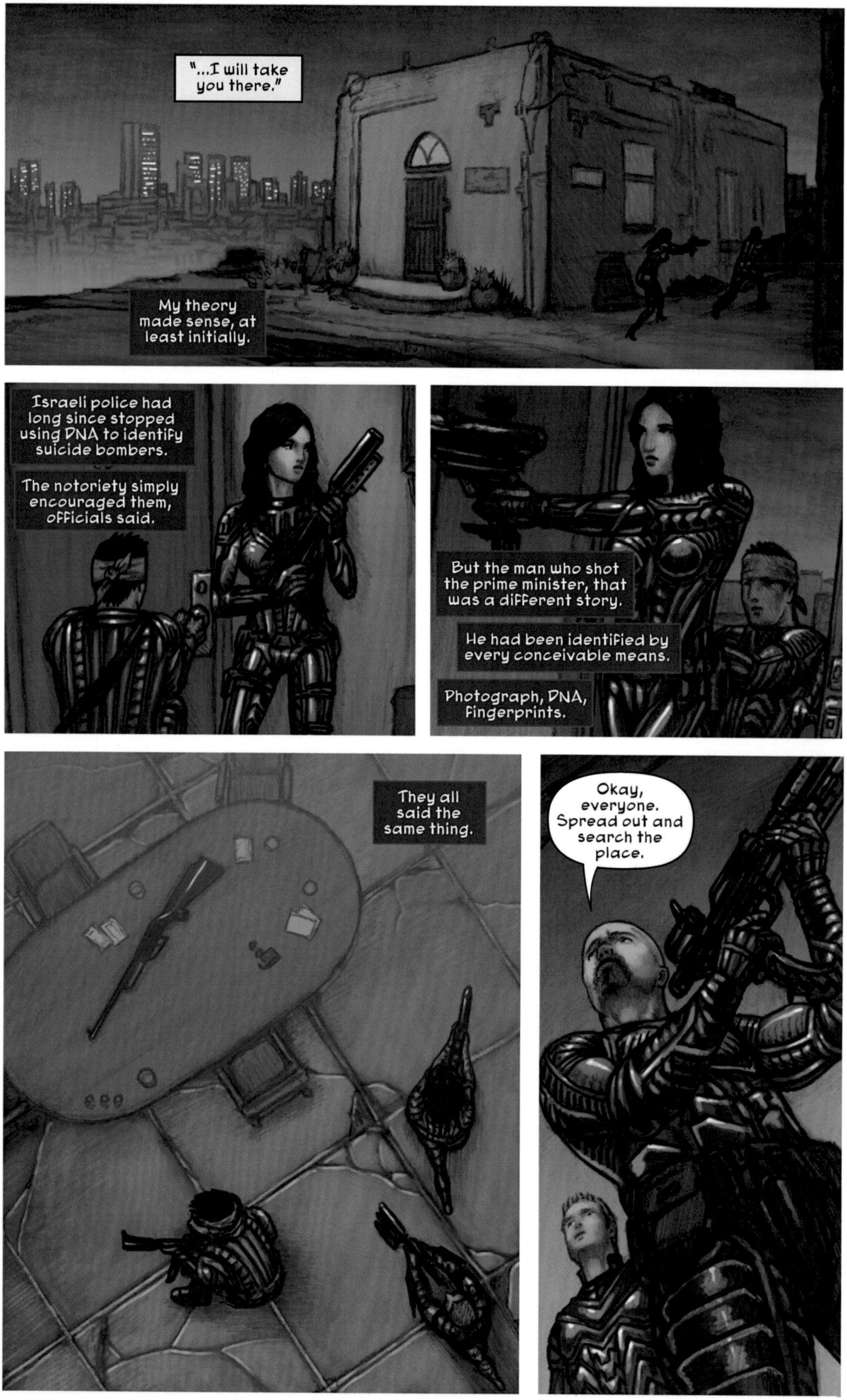
"...I will take you there."
My theory made sense, at least initially.
Israeli police had long since stopped using DNA to identify suicide bombers.
The notoriety simply encouraged them, officials said.
But the man who shot the prime minister, that was a different story.
He had been identified by every conceivable means.
Photograph, DNA, fingerprints.
They all said the same thing.
Okay, everyone. Spread out and search the place.

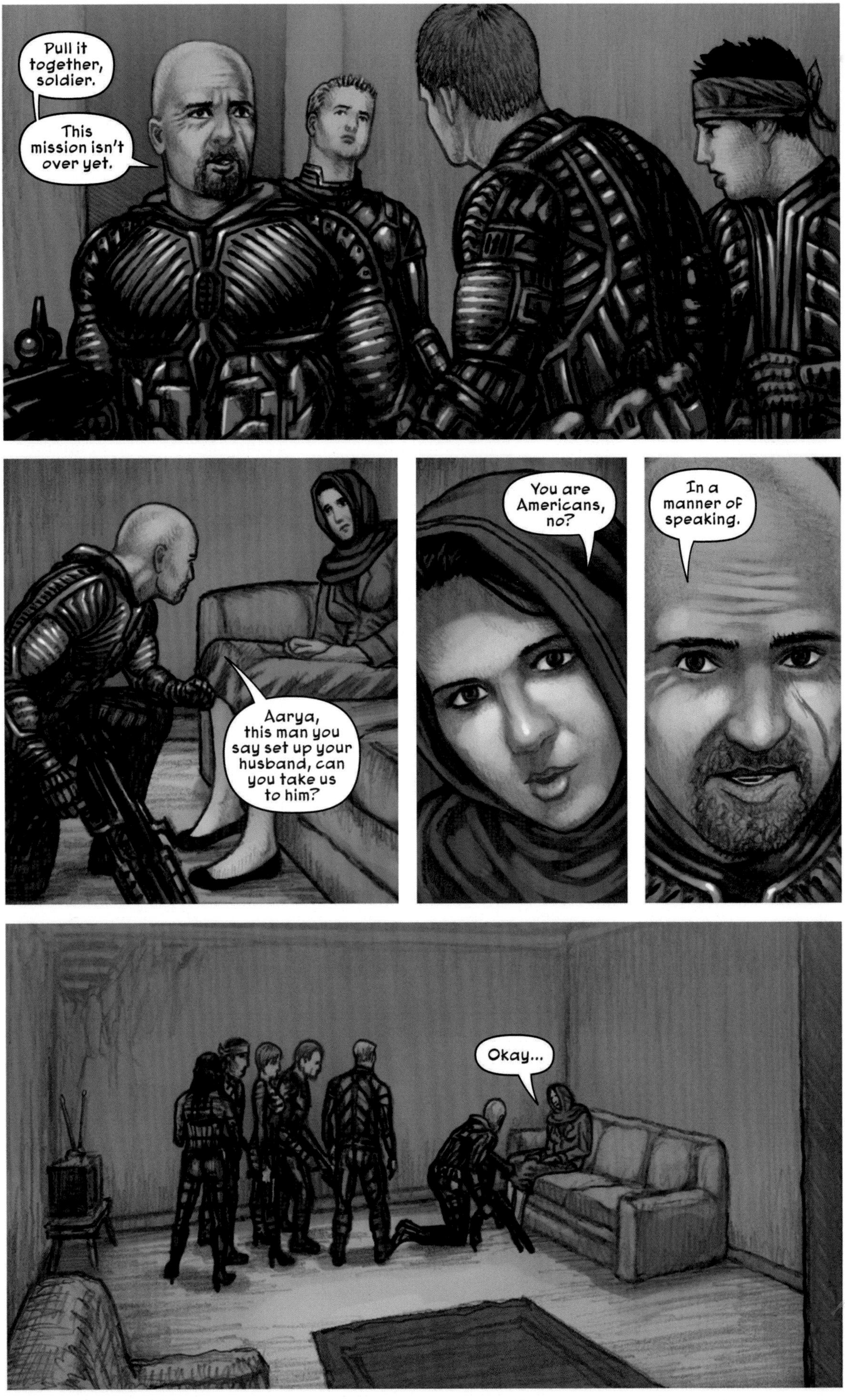
Pull it together, soldier.
This mission isn't over yet.
Aarya, this man you say set up your husband, can you take us to him?
You are Americans, no?
In a manner of speaking.
Okay...

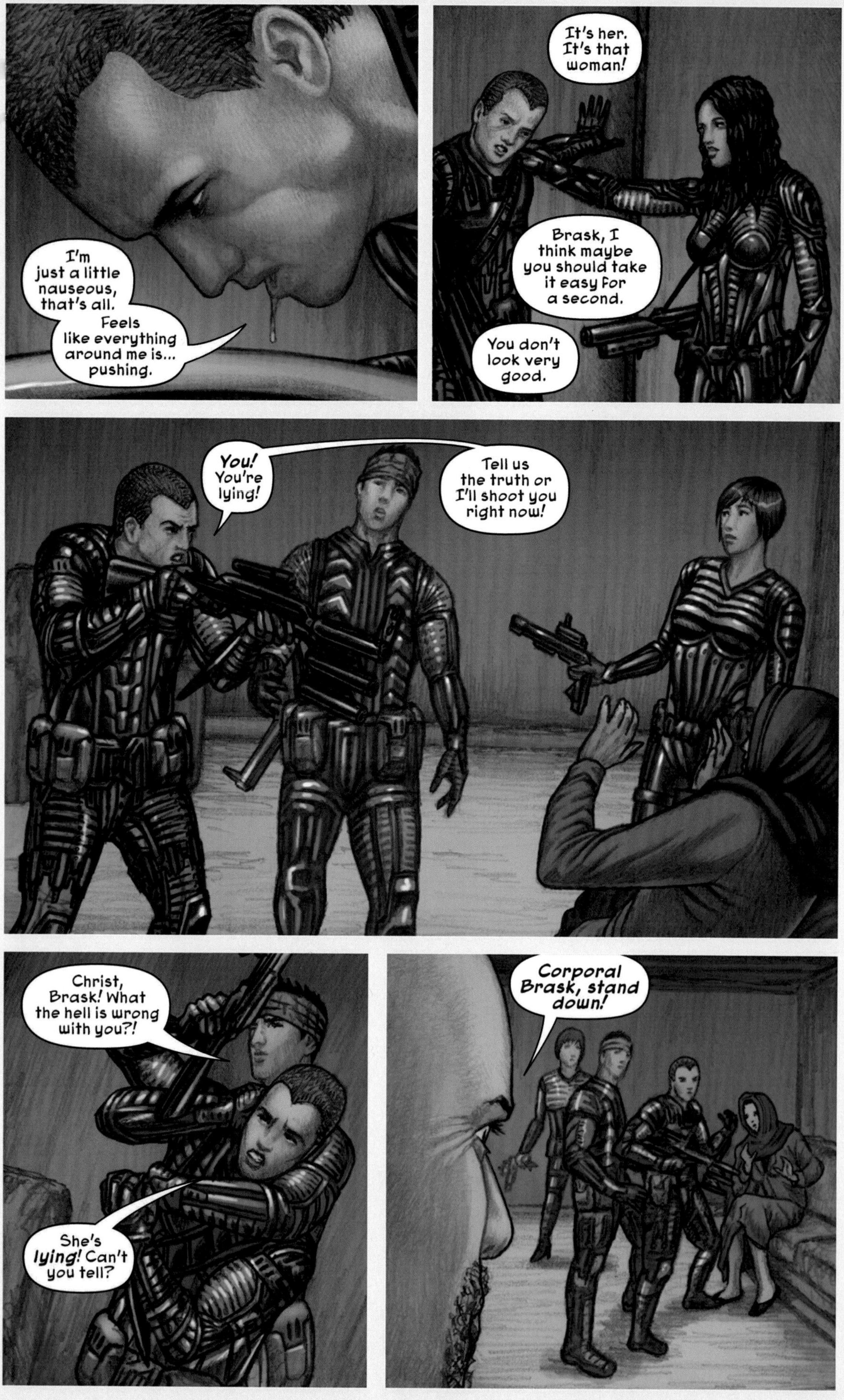
I'm just a little nauseous, that's all.
Feels like everything around me is... pushing.
It's her. It's that woman!
Brask, I think maybe you should take it easy for a second.
You don't look very good.
You! You're lying!
Tell us the truth or I'll shoot you right now!
Christ, Brask! What the hell is wrong with you?!
She's lying! Can't you tell?
Corporal Brask, stand down!

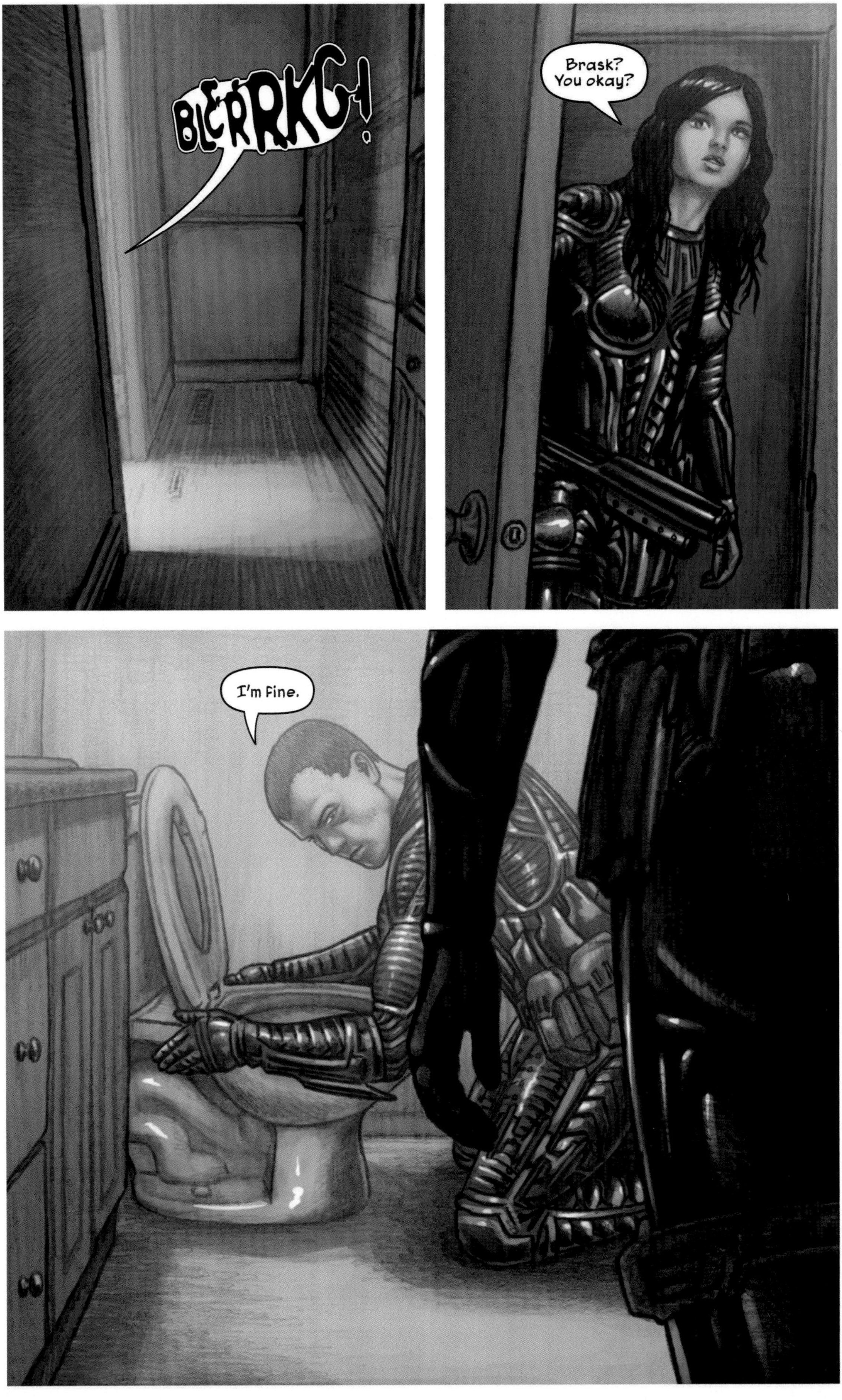
BLERRKG!
Brask? You okay?
I'm fine.

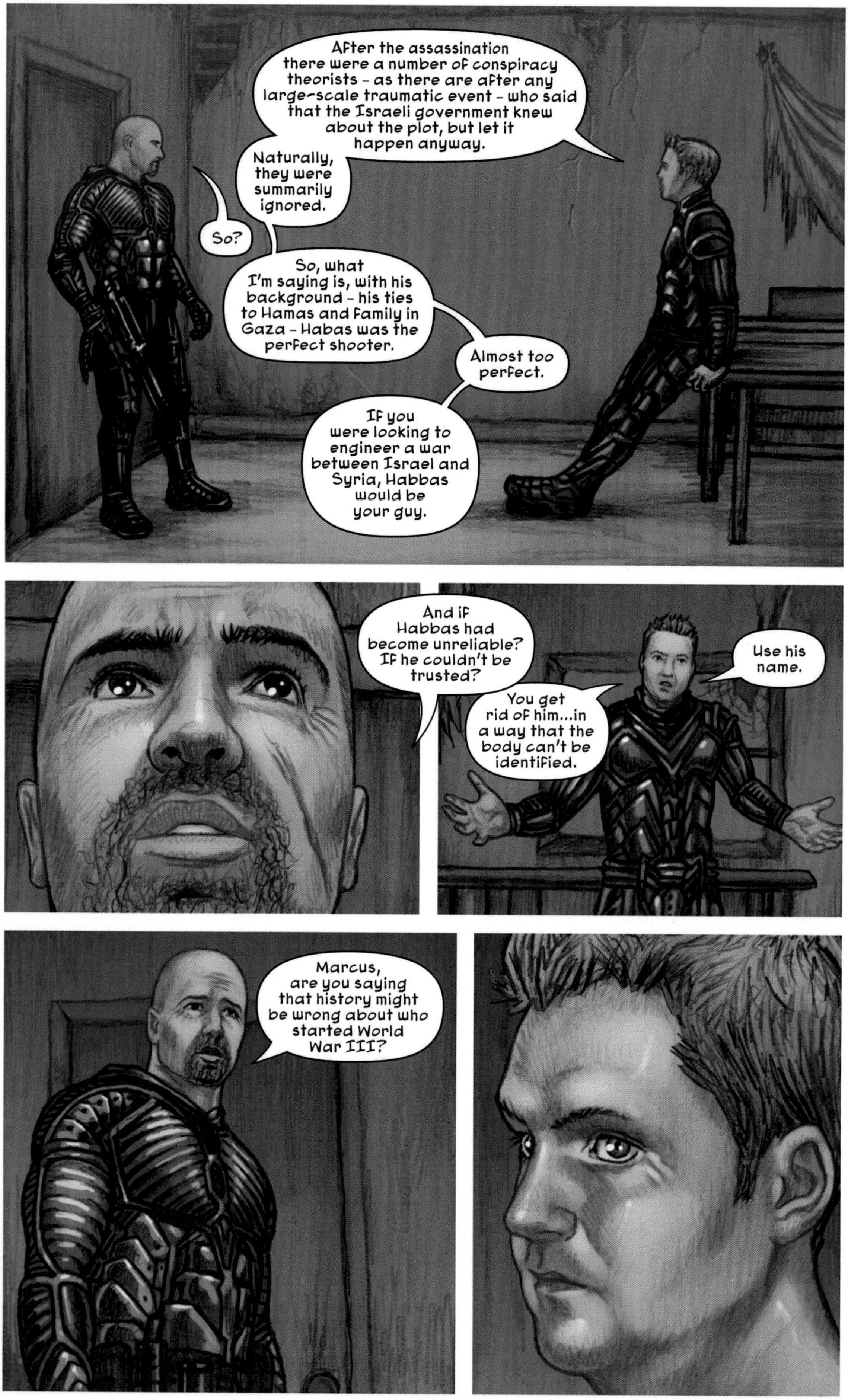
After the assassination there were a number of conspiracy theorists – as there are after any large-scale traumatic event – who said that the Israeli government knew about the plot, but let it happen anyway.
Naturally, they were summarily ignored.
So?
So, what I'm saying is, with his background – his ties to Hamas and family in Gaza – Habas was the perfect shooter.
Almost too perfect.
If you were looking to engineer a war between Israel and Syria, Habbas would be your guy.
And if Habbas had become unreliable? If he couldn't be trusted?
You get rid of him...in a way that the body can't be identified.
Use his name.
Marcus, are you saying that history might be wrong about who started World War III?

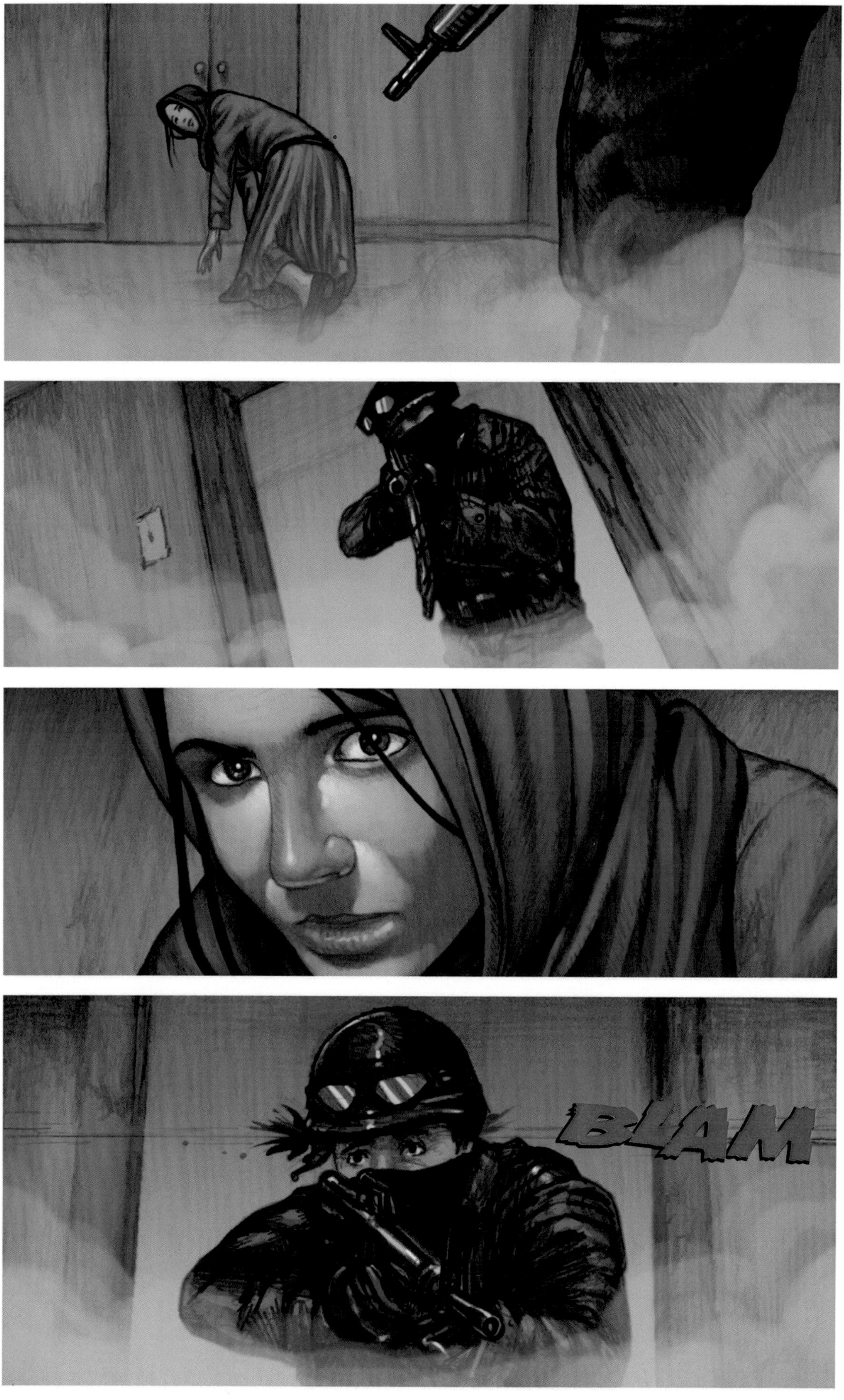
BLAM

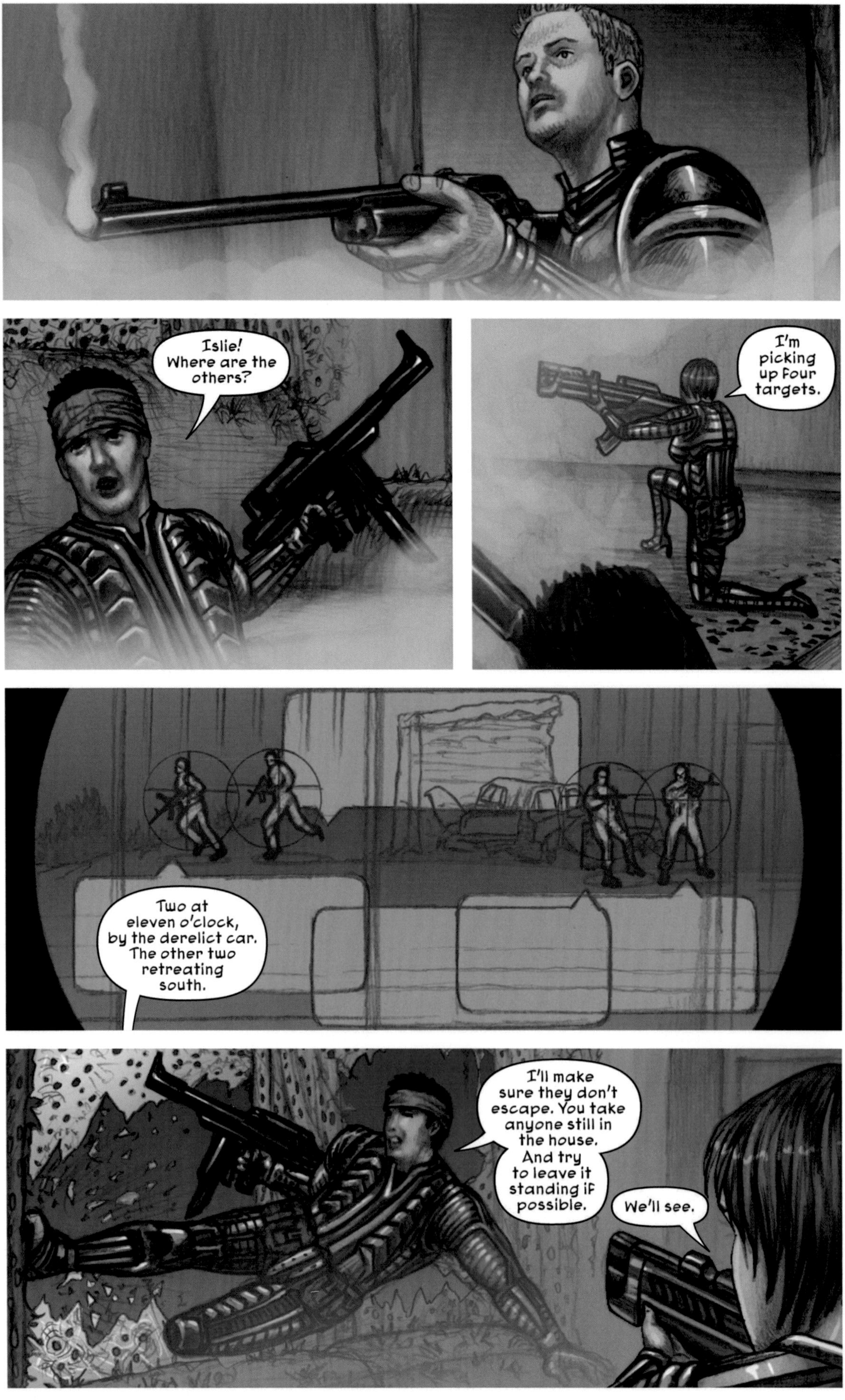
Islie! Where are the others?
I'm picking up four targets.
Two at eleven o'clock, by the derelict car. The other two retreating south.
I'll make sure they don't escape. You take anyone still in the house. And try to leave it standing if possible.
We'll see.

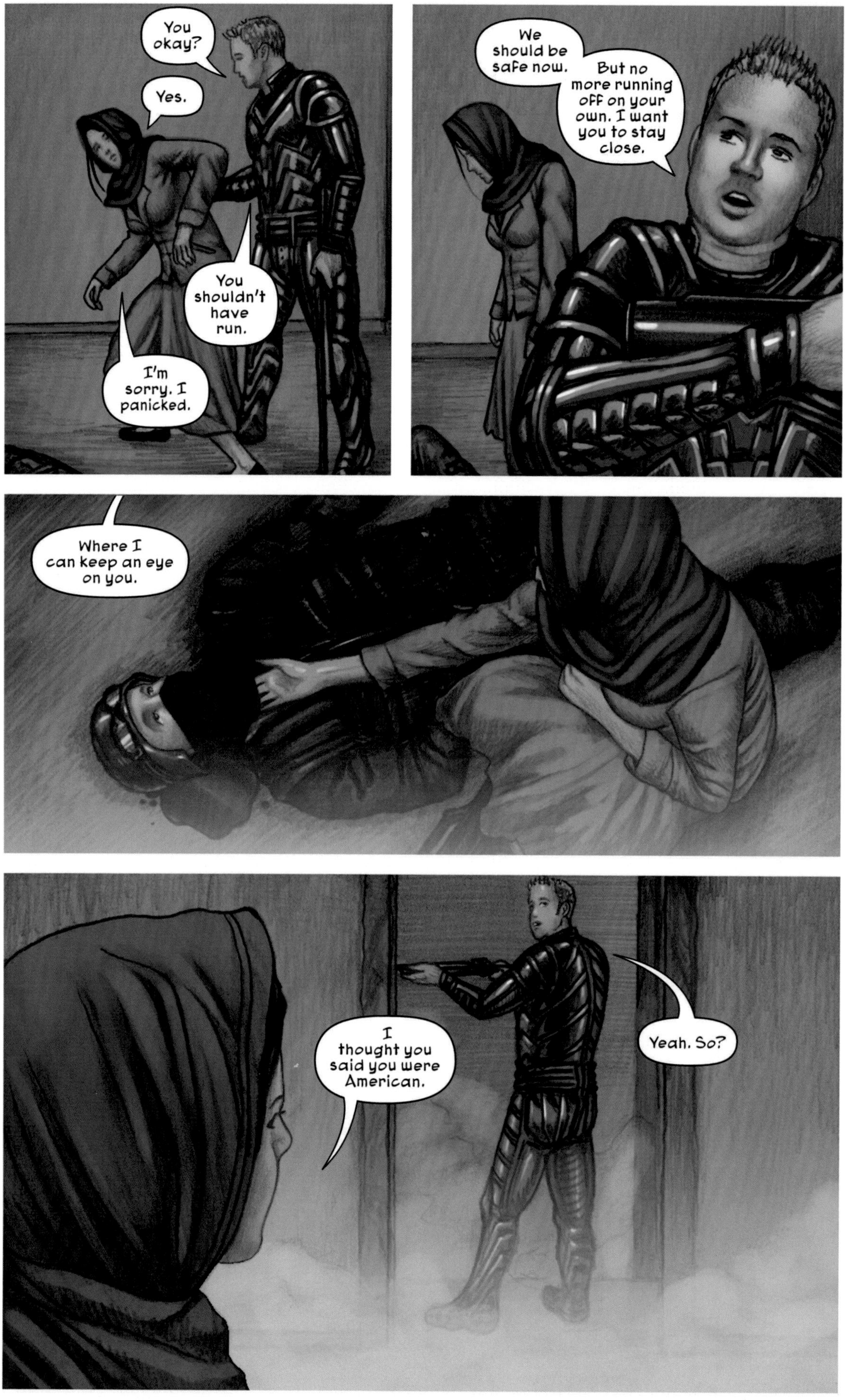
You okay?
Yes.
You shouldn't have run.
I'm sorry. I panicked.
We should be safe now.
But no more running off on your own. I want you to stay close.
Where I can keep an eye on you.
I thought you said you were American.
Yeah. So?

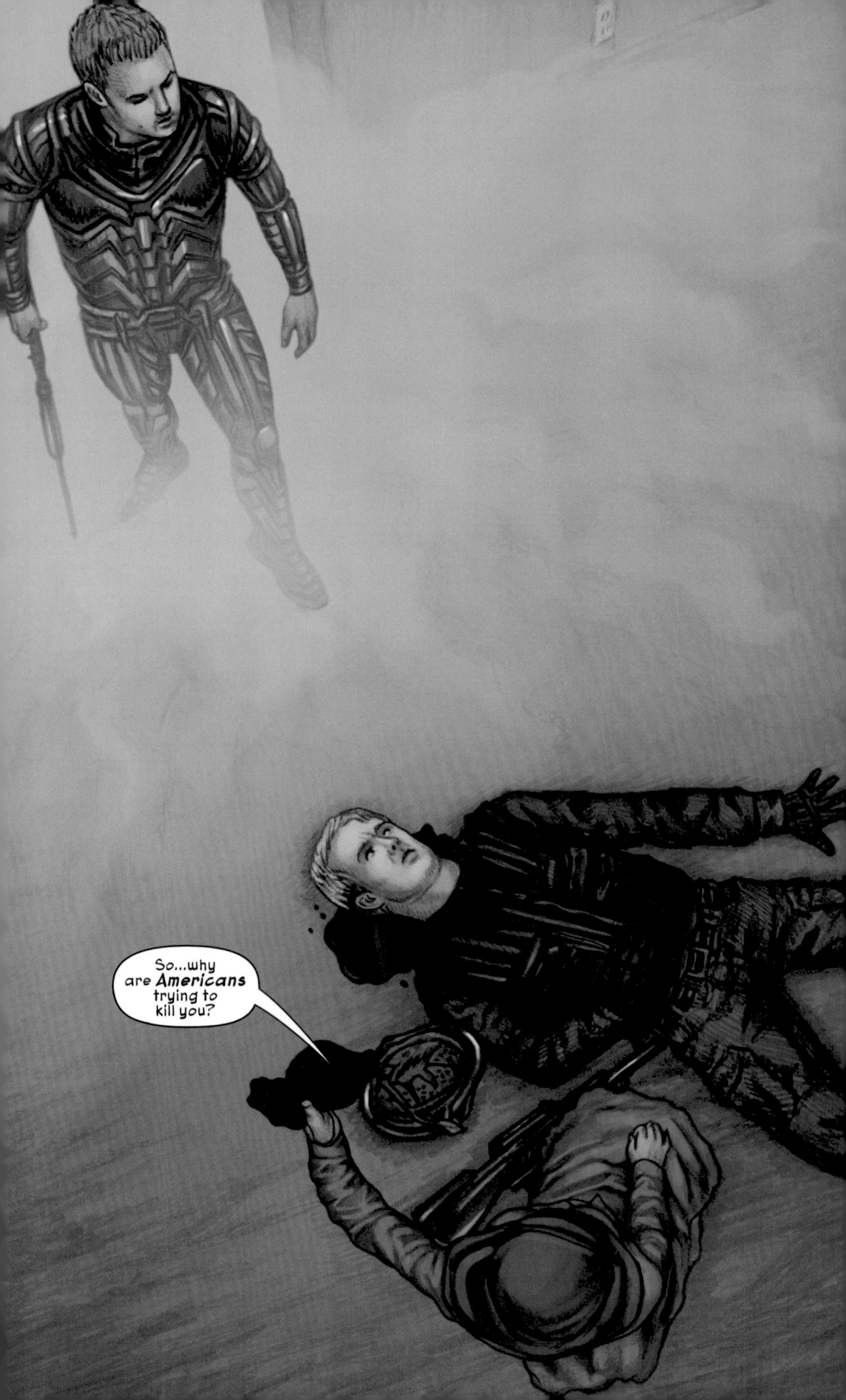
So...why are Americans trying to kill you?

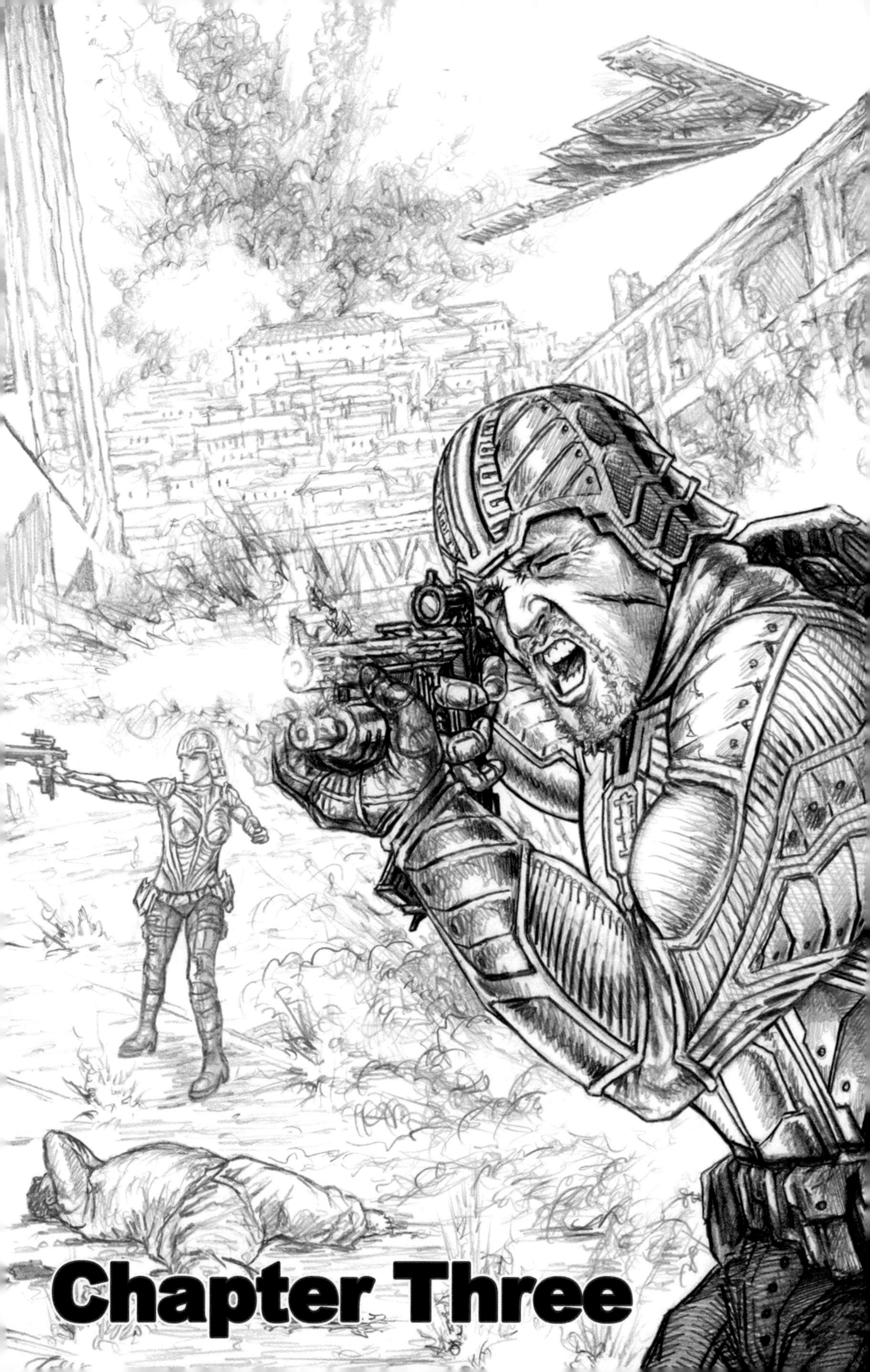

Chapter Three

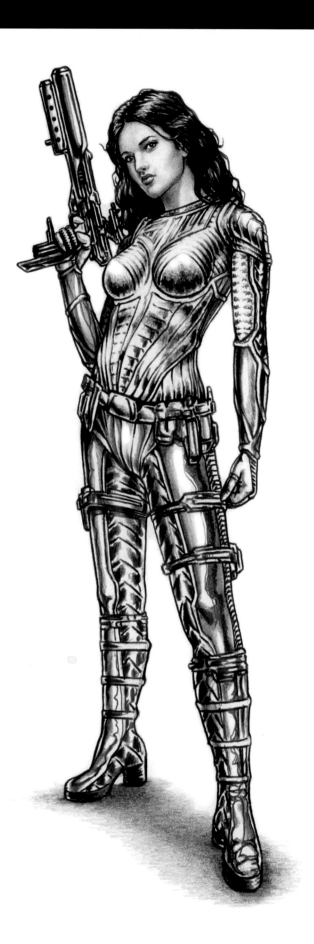

"KENRA"

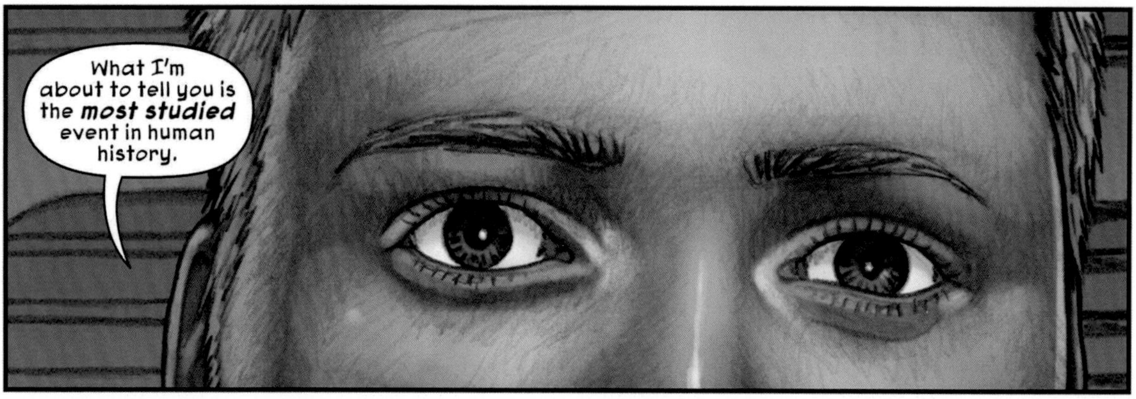
What I'm about to tell you is the *most studied* event in human history.

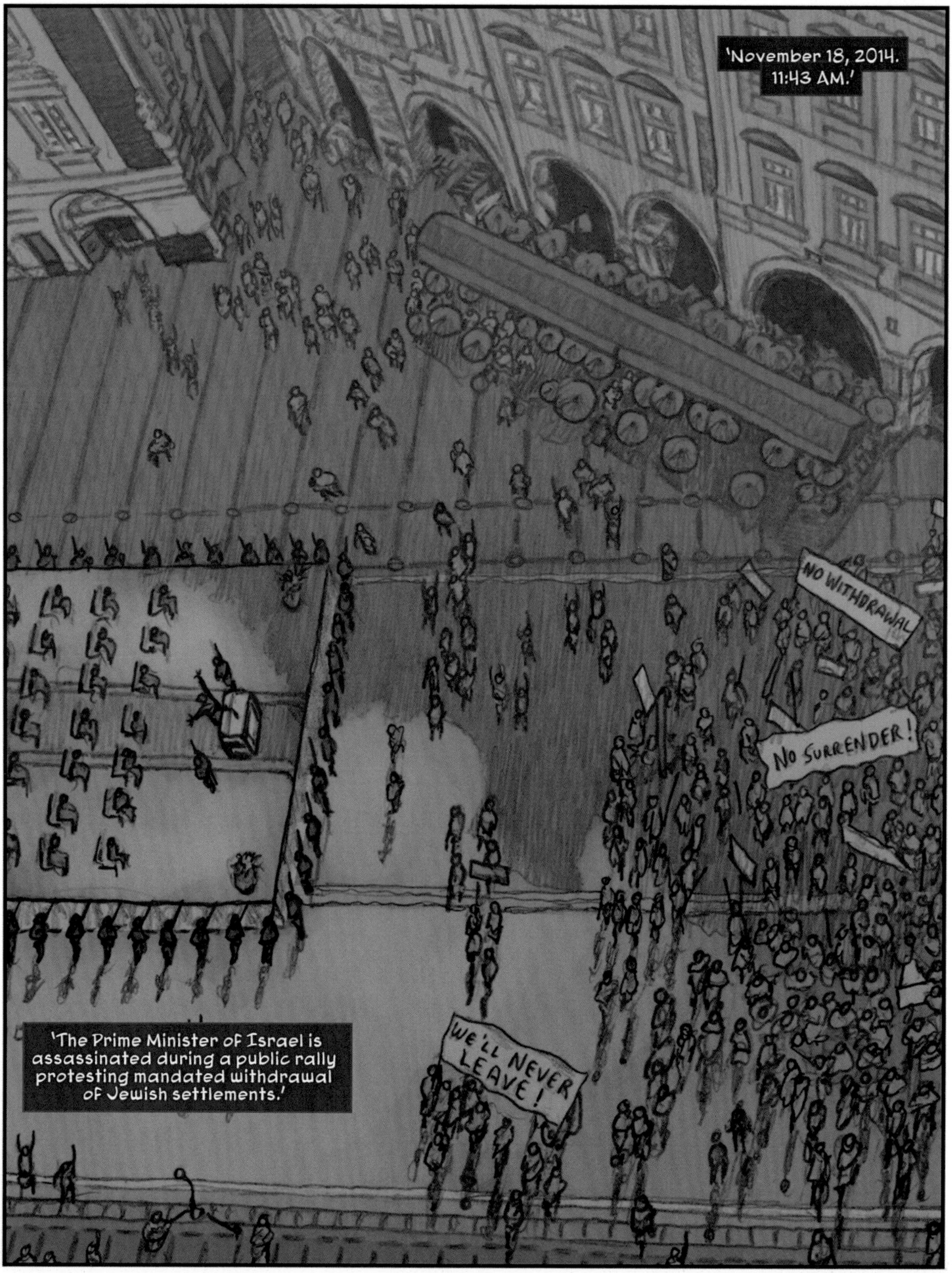
'November 18, 2014. 11:43 AM.'
NO WITHDRAWAL
NO SURRENDER!
WE'LL NEVER LEAVE!
'The Prime Minister of Israel is assassinated during a public rally protesting mandated withdrawal of Jewish settlements.'

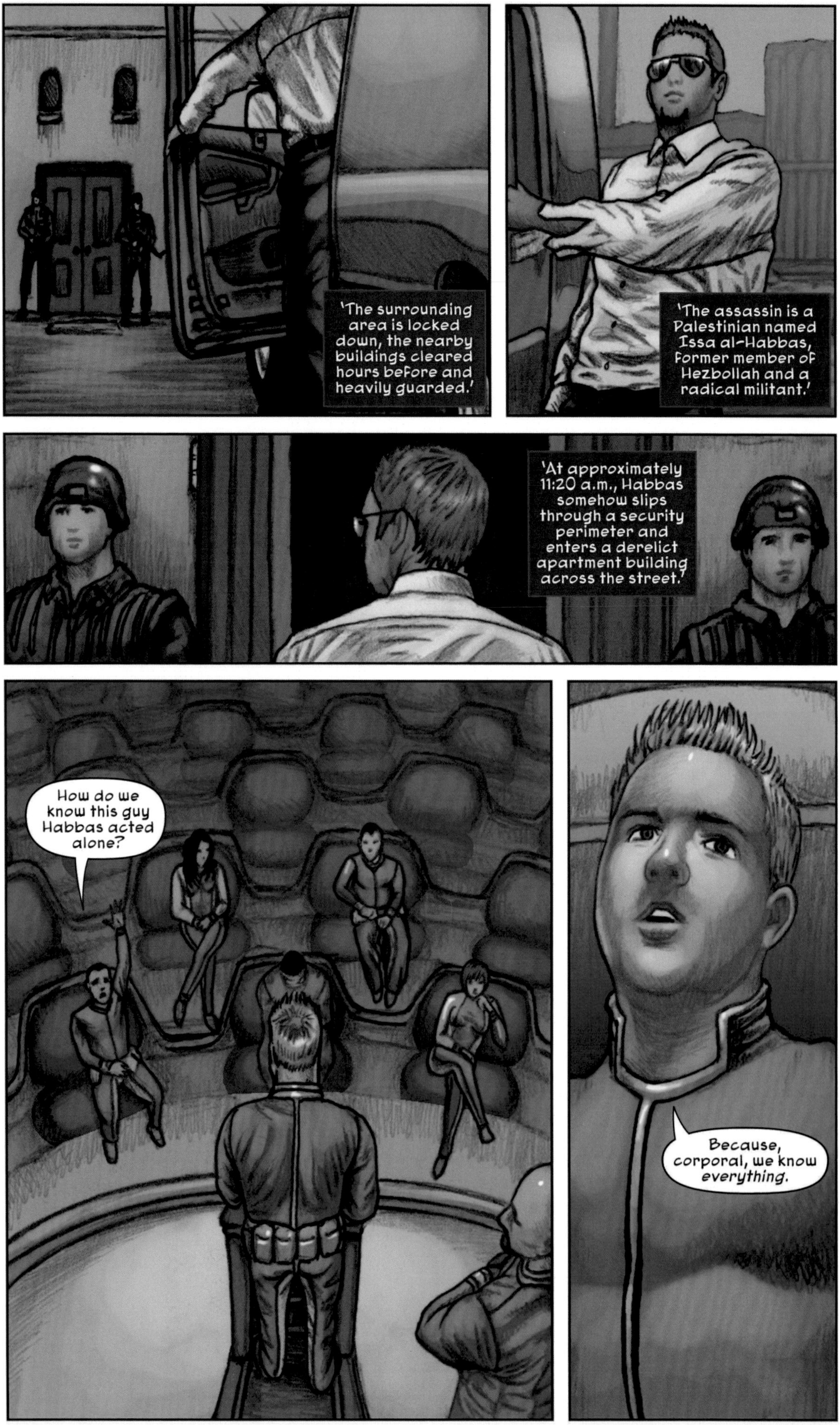
'The surrounding area is locked down, the nearby buildings cleared hours before and heavily guarded.'
'The assassin is a Palestinian named Issa al-Habbas, former member of Hezbollah and a radical militant.'
'At approximately 11:20 a.m., Habbas somehow slips through a security perimeter and enters a derelict apartment building across the street.'
How do we know this guy Habbas acted alone?
Because, corporal, we know *everything*.

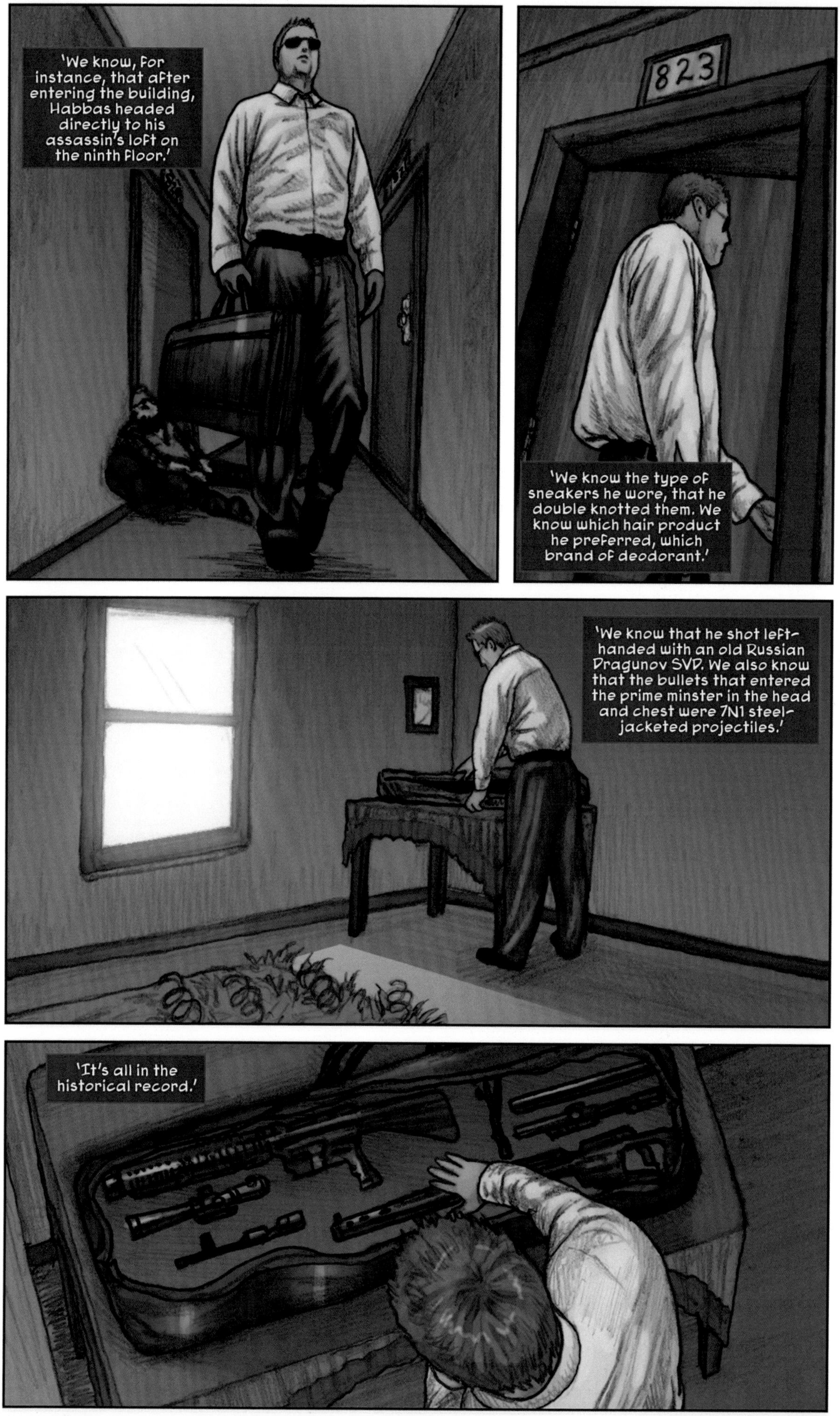
'We know, for instance, that after entering the building, Habbas headed directly to his assassin's loft on the ninth floor.'
823
'We know the type of sneakers he wore, that he double knotted them. We know which hair product he preferred, which brand of deodorant.'
'We know that he shot left-handed with an old Russian Dragunov SVD. We also know that the bullets that entered the prime minster in the head and chest were 7N1 steel-jacketed projectiles.'
'It's all in the historical record.'

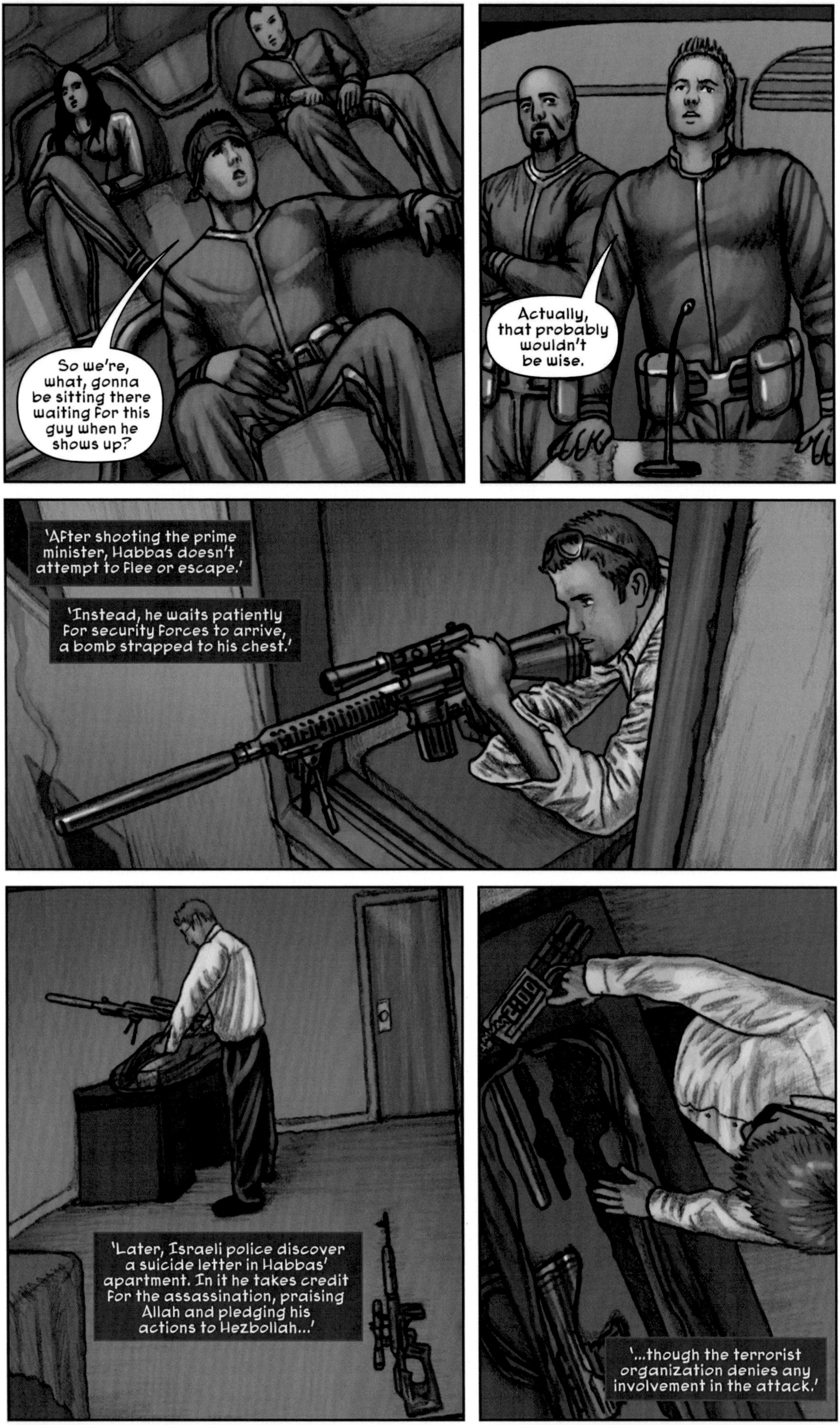
So we're, what, gonna be sitting there waiting for this guy when he shows up?
Actually, that probably wouldn't be wise.
'After shooting the prime minister, Habbas doesn't attempt to flee or escape.'
'Instead, he waits patiently for security forces to arrive, a bomb strapped to his chest.'
'Later, Israeli police discover a suicide letter in Habbas' apartment. In it he takes credit for the assassination, praising Allah and pledging his actions to Hezbollah...'
'...though the terrorist organization denies any involvement in the attack.'

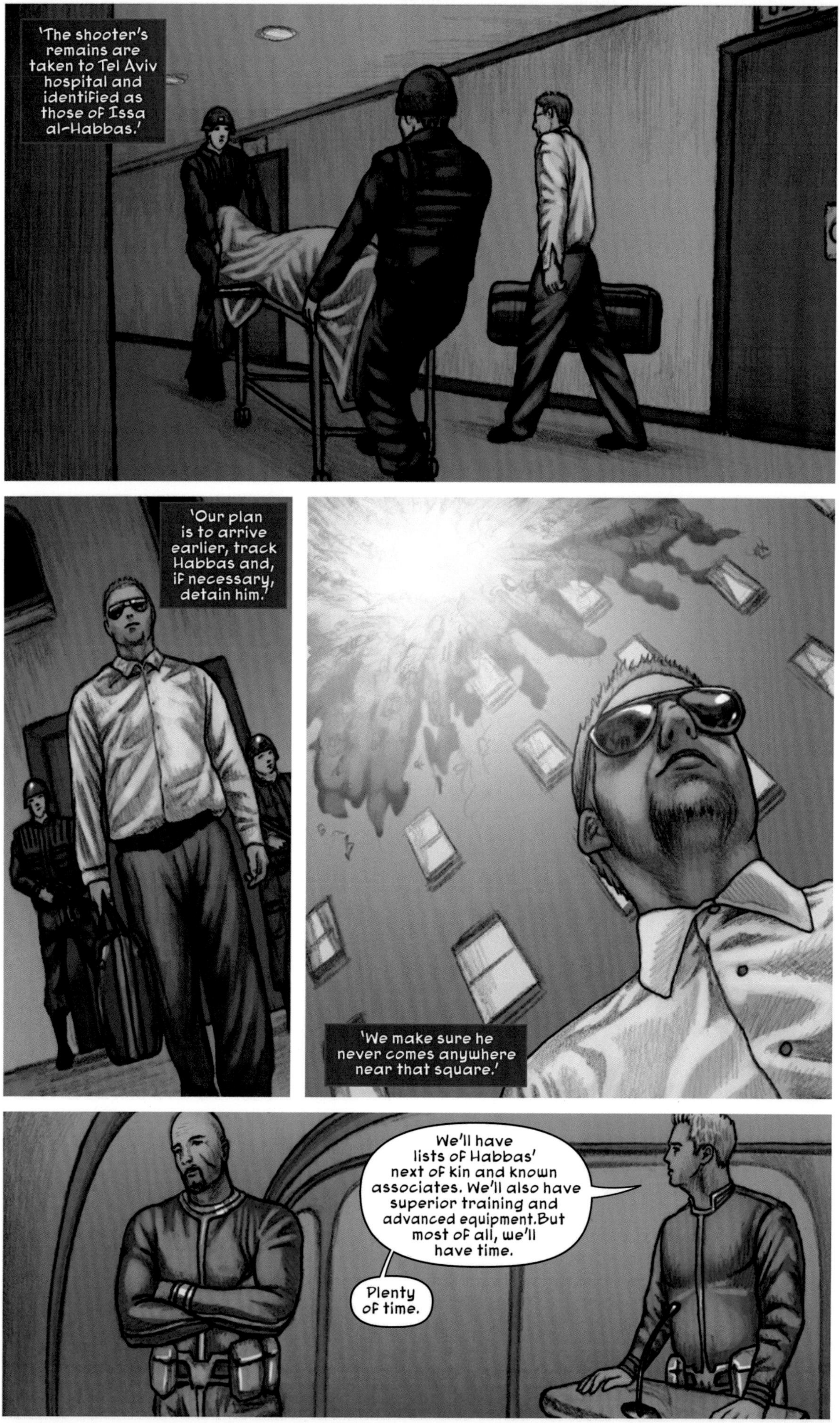
'The shooter's remains are taken to Tel Aviv hospital and identified as those of Issa al-Habbas.'
'Our plan is to arrive earlier, track Habbas and, if necessary, detain him.'
'We make sure he never comes anywhere near that square.'
We'll have lists of Habbas' next of kin and known associates. We'll also have superior training and advanced equipment. But most of all, we'll have time.
Plenty of time.

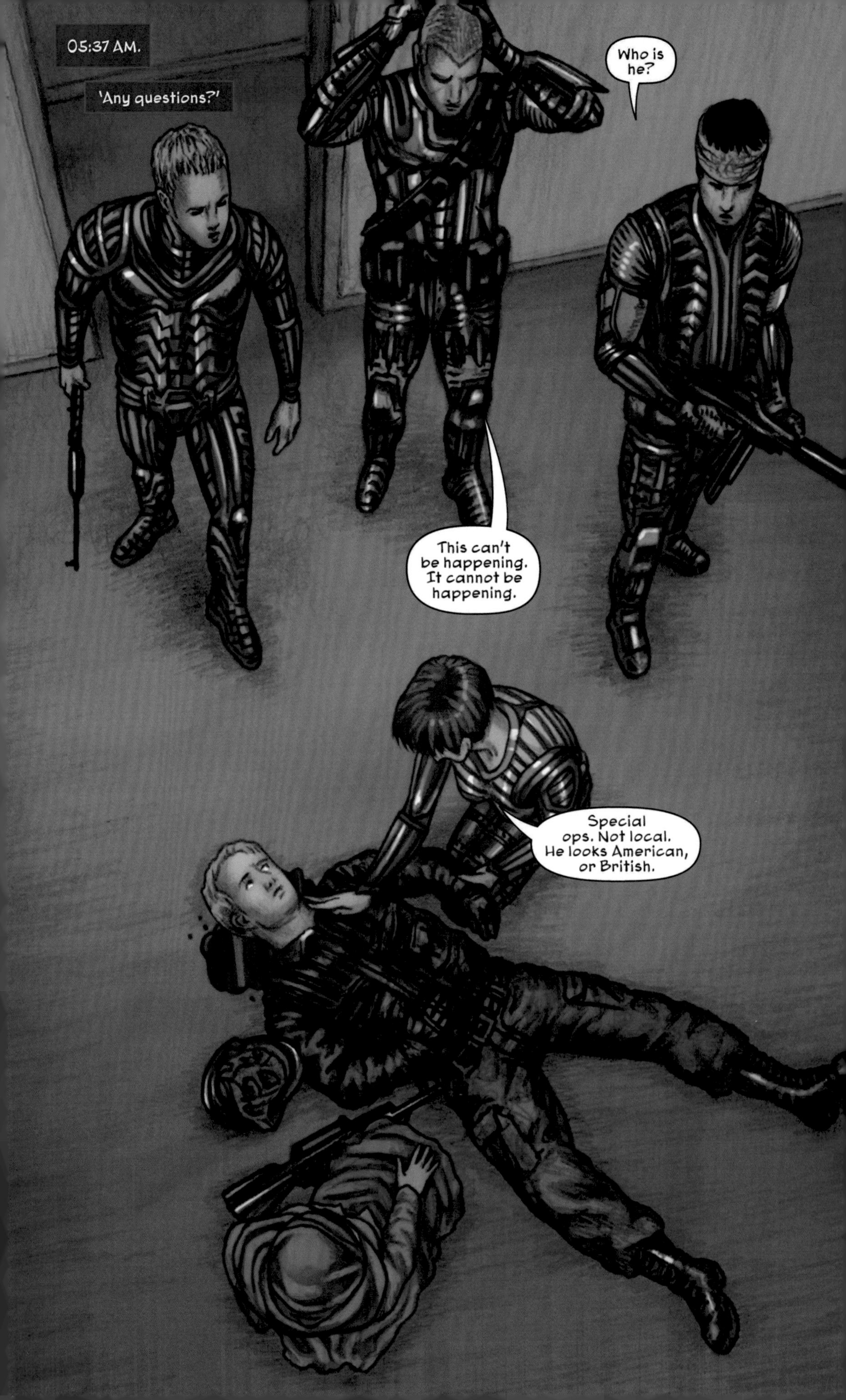
05:37 AM.
'Any questions?'
Who is he?
This can't be happening. It cannot be happening.
Special ops. Not local. He looks American, or British.

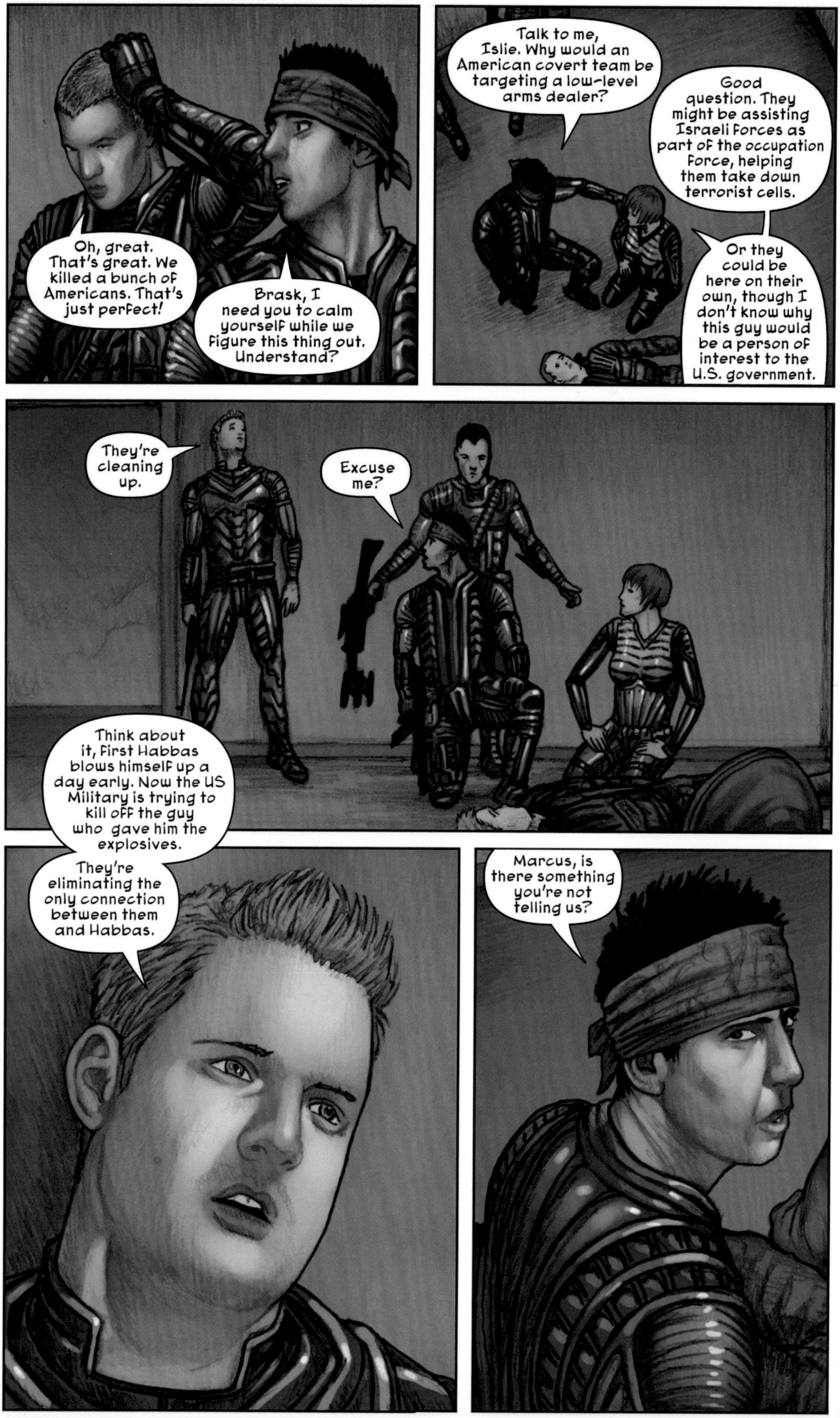
Oh, great. That's great. We killed a bunch of Americans. That's just perfect!
Brask, I need you to calm yourself while we figure this thing out. Understand?
Talk to me, Islie. Why would an American covert team be targeting a low-level arms dealer?
Good question. They might be assisting Israeli forces as part of the occupation force, helping them take down terrorist cells.
Or they could be here on their own, though I don't know why this guy would be a person of interest to the U.S. government.
They're cleaning up.
Excuse me?
Think about it, first Habbas blows himself up a day early. Now the US Military is trying to kill off the guy who gave him the explosives.
They're eliminating the only connection between them and Habbas.
Marcus, is there something you're not telling us?

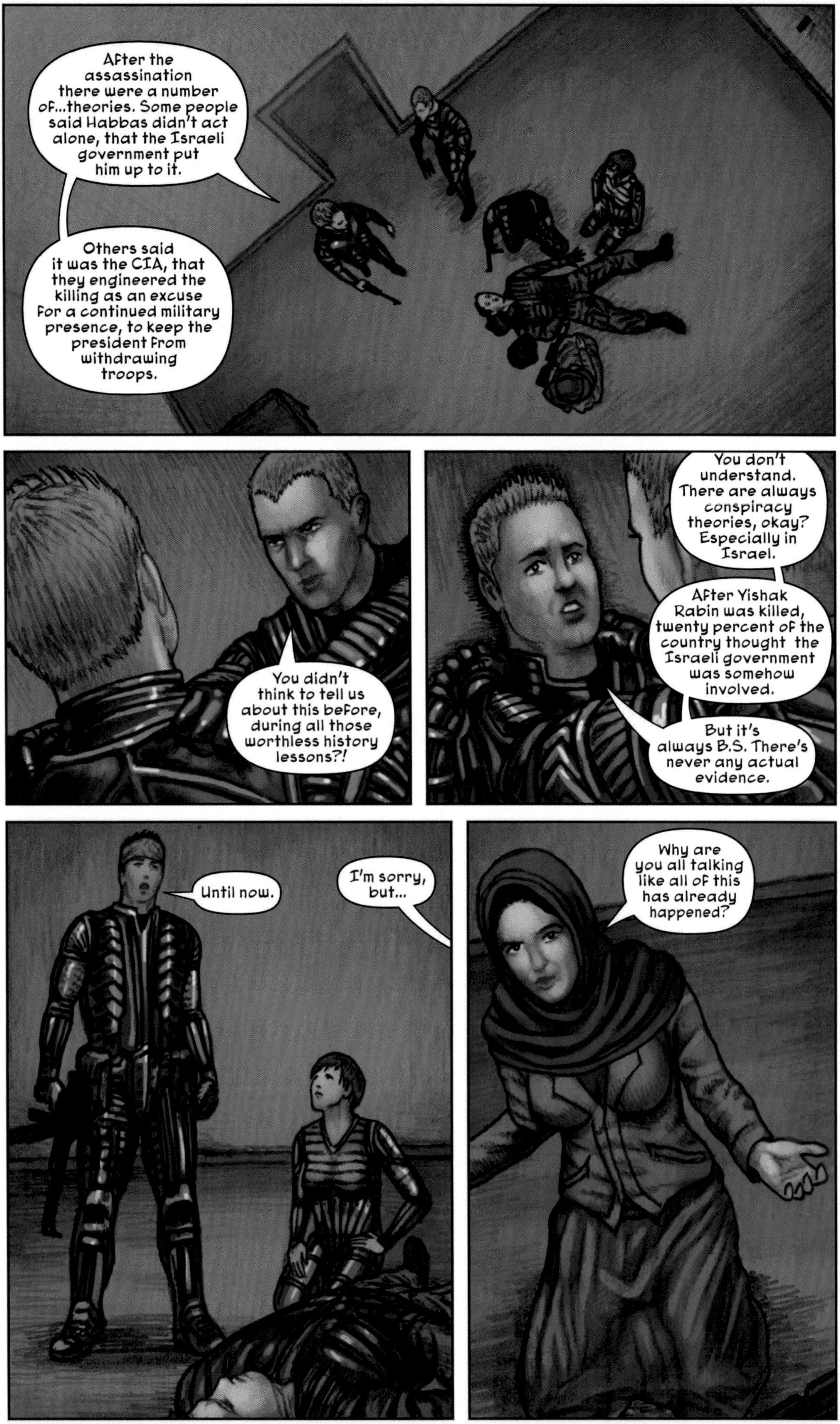
After the assassination there were a number of...theories. Some people said Habbas didn't act alone, that the Israeli government put him up to it.
Others said it was the CIA, that they engineered the killing as an excuse for a continued military presence, to keep the president from withdrawing troops.
You didn't think to tell us about this before, during all those worthless history lessons?!
You don't understand. There are always conspiracy theories, okay? Especially in Israel.
After Yishak Rabin was killed, twenty percent of the country thought the Israeli government was somehow involved.
But it's always B.S. There's never any actual evidence.
Until now.
I'm sorry, but...
Why are you all talking like all of this has already happened?

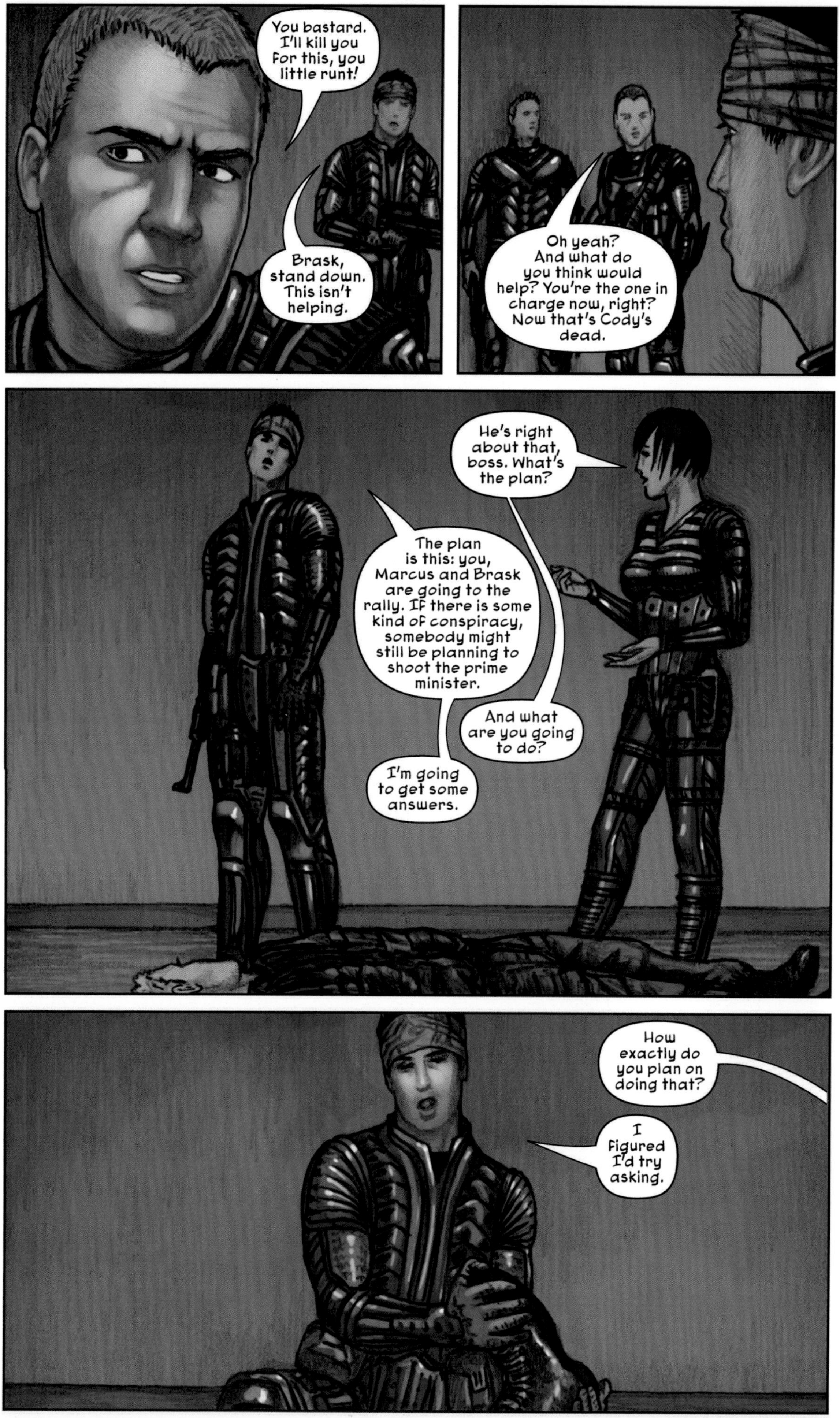
You bastard. I'll kill you for this, you little runt!
Brask, stand down. This isn't helping.
Oh yeah? And what do you think would help? You're the one in charge now, right? Now that's Cody's dead.
He's right about that, boss. What's the plan?
The plan is this: you, Marcus and Brask are going to the rally. If there is some kind of conspiracy, somebody might still be planning to shoot the prime minister.
And what are you going to do?
I'm going to get some answers.
How exactly do you plan on doing that?
I figured I'd try asking.

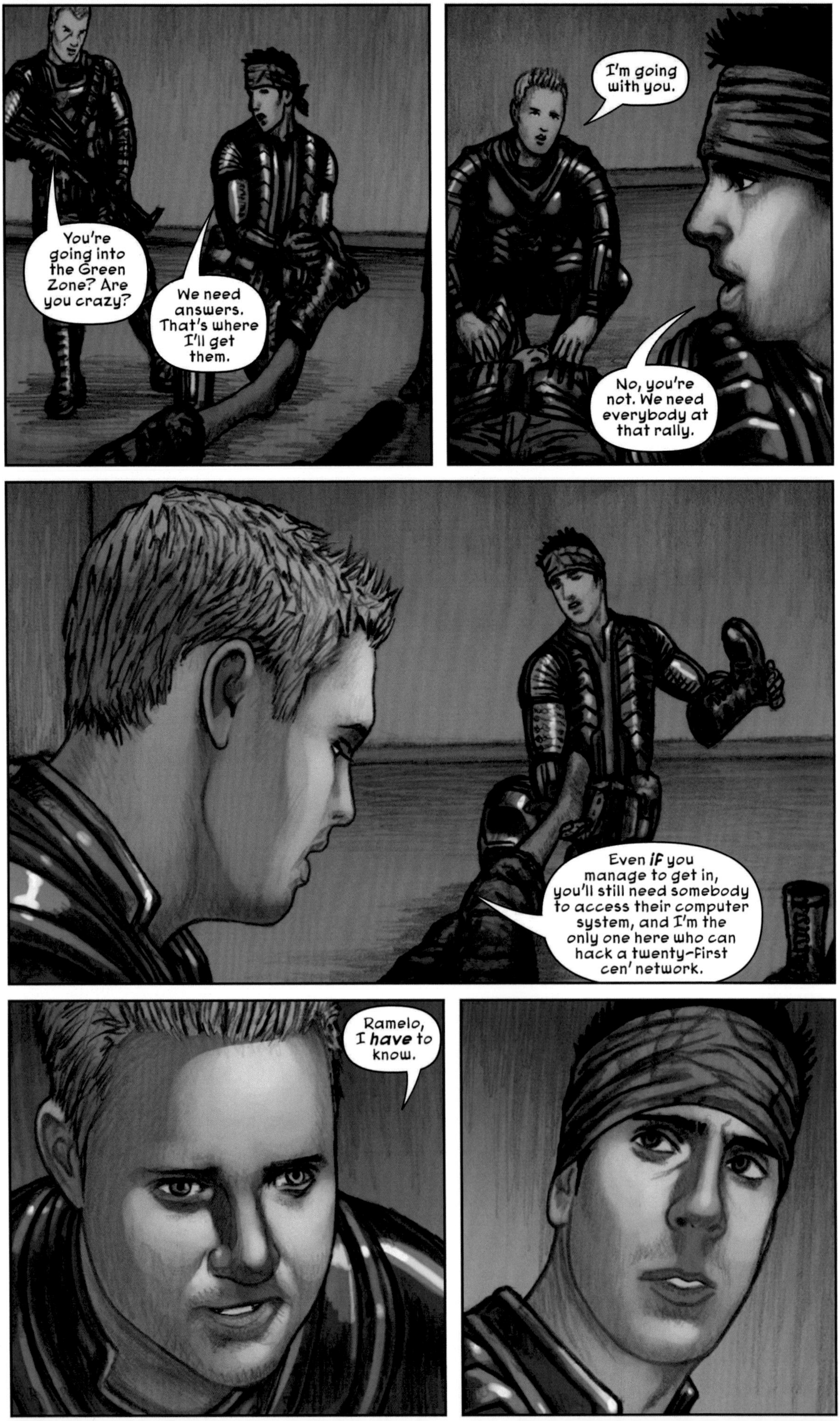
You're going into the Green Zone? Are you crazy?
We need answers. That's where I'll get them.
I'm going with you.
No, you're not. We need everybody at that rally.
Even *if* you manage to get in, you'll still need somebody to access their computer system, and I'm the only one here who can hack a twenty-first cen' network.
Ramelo, I *have* to know.

Fine. Look around. See if one of these soldiers fits your size.

This whole thing is insane! This isn't our past. We never made it out of that black hole! Have you ever thought about that?

I don't know what's going on here. You all sound like crazy people.

But I'm not leaving your side. Not again.

It'll be too dangerous where we're going.

Please, I want to help. These people set up my husband.

Okay, I think I have an idea how to get us in, and it involves a third person.

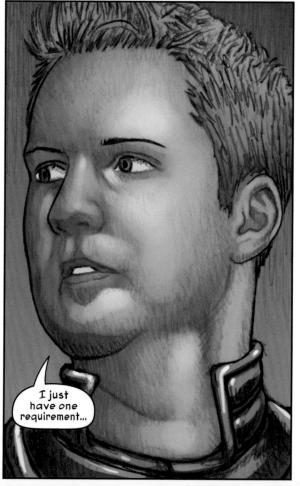

I just have one requirement...

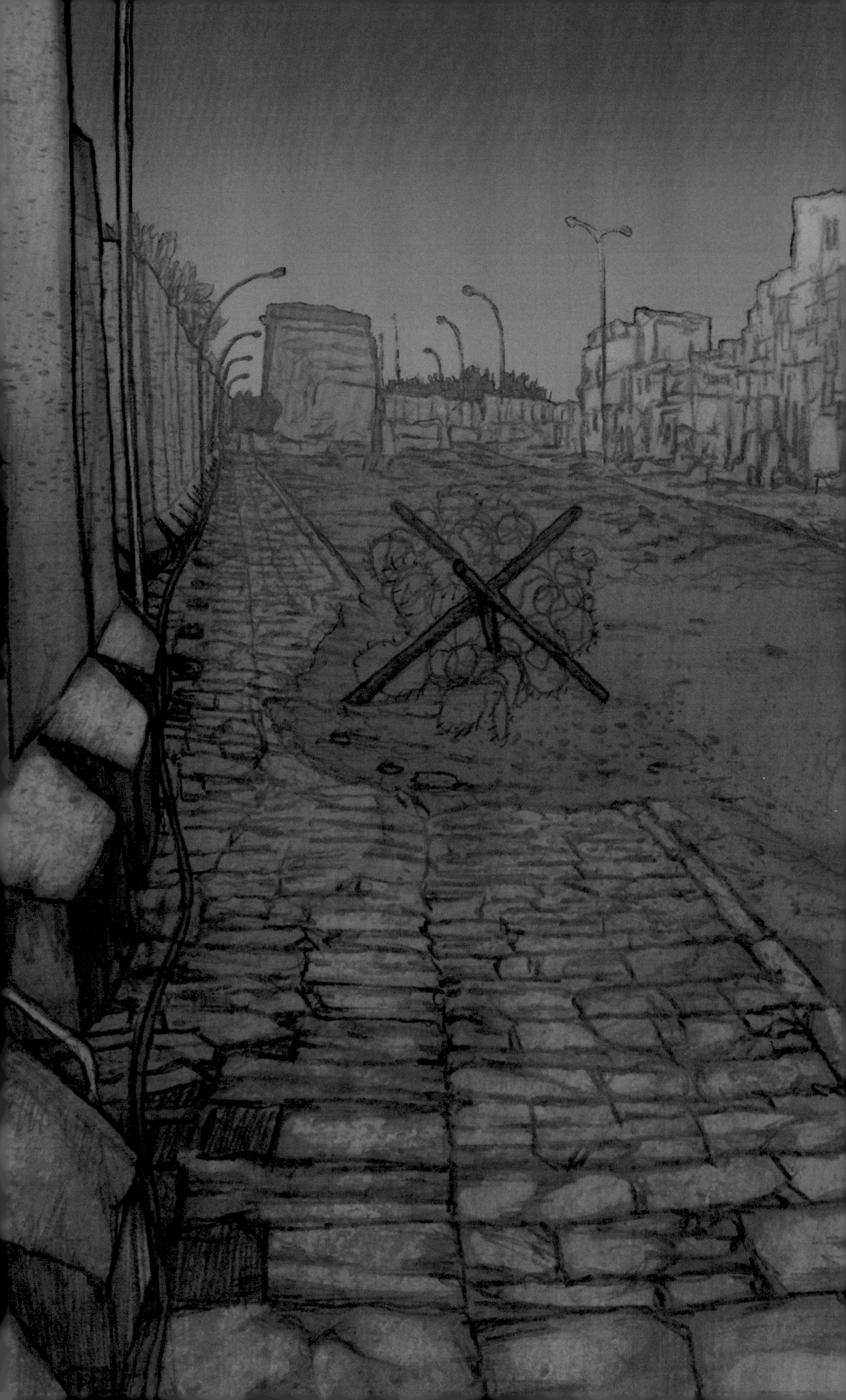

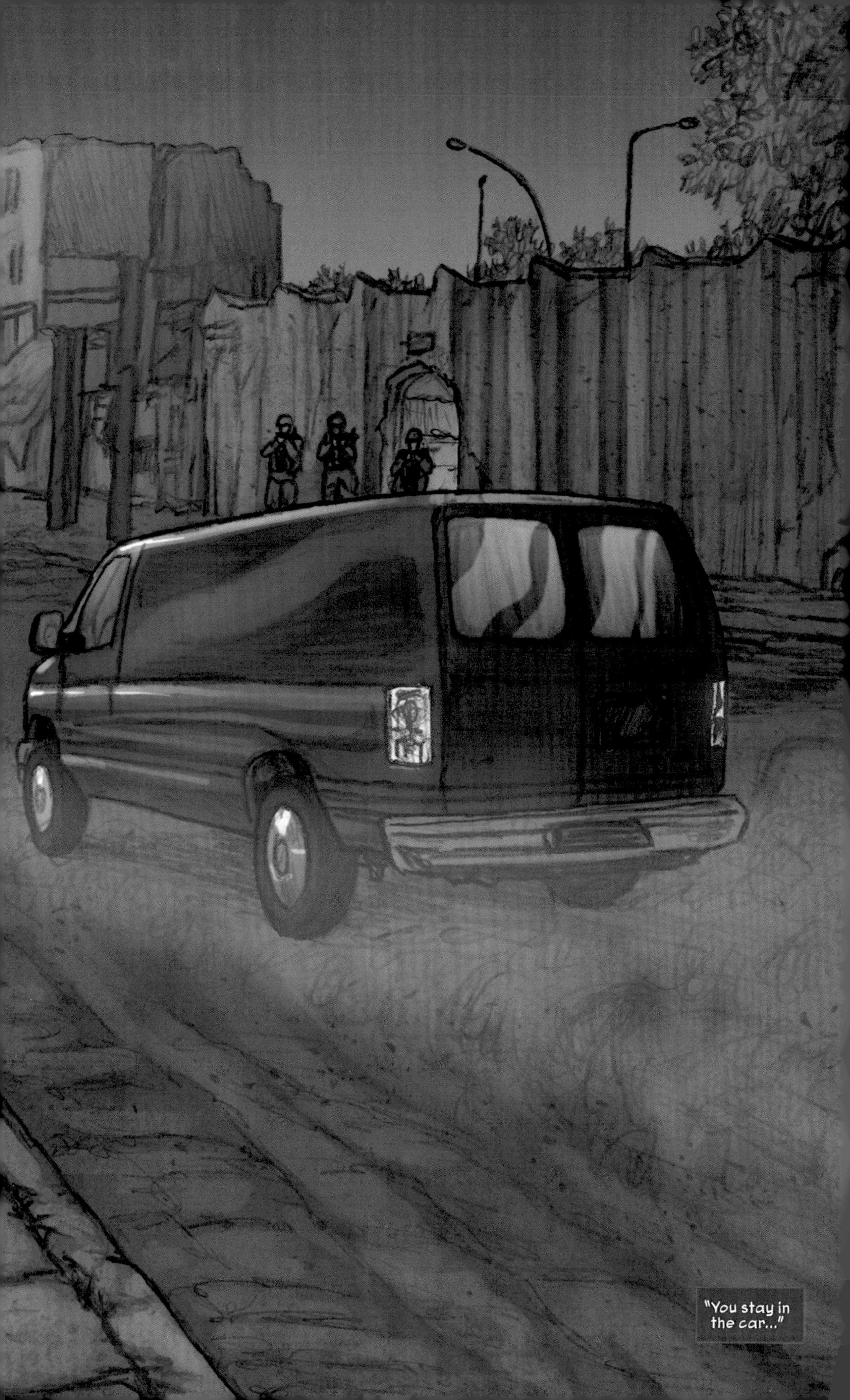
"You stay in the car..."

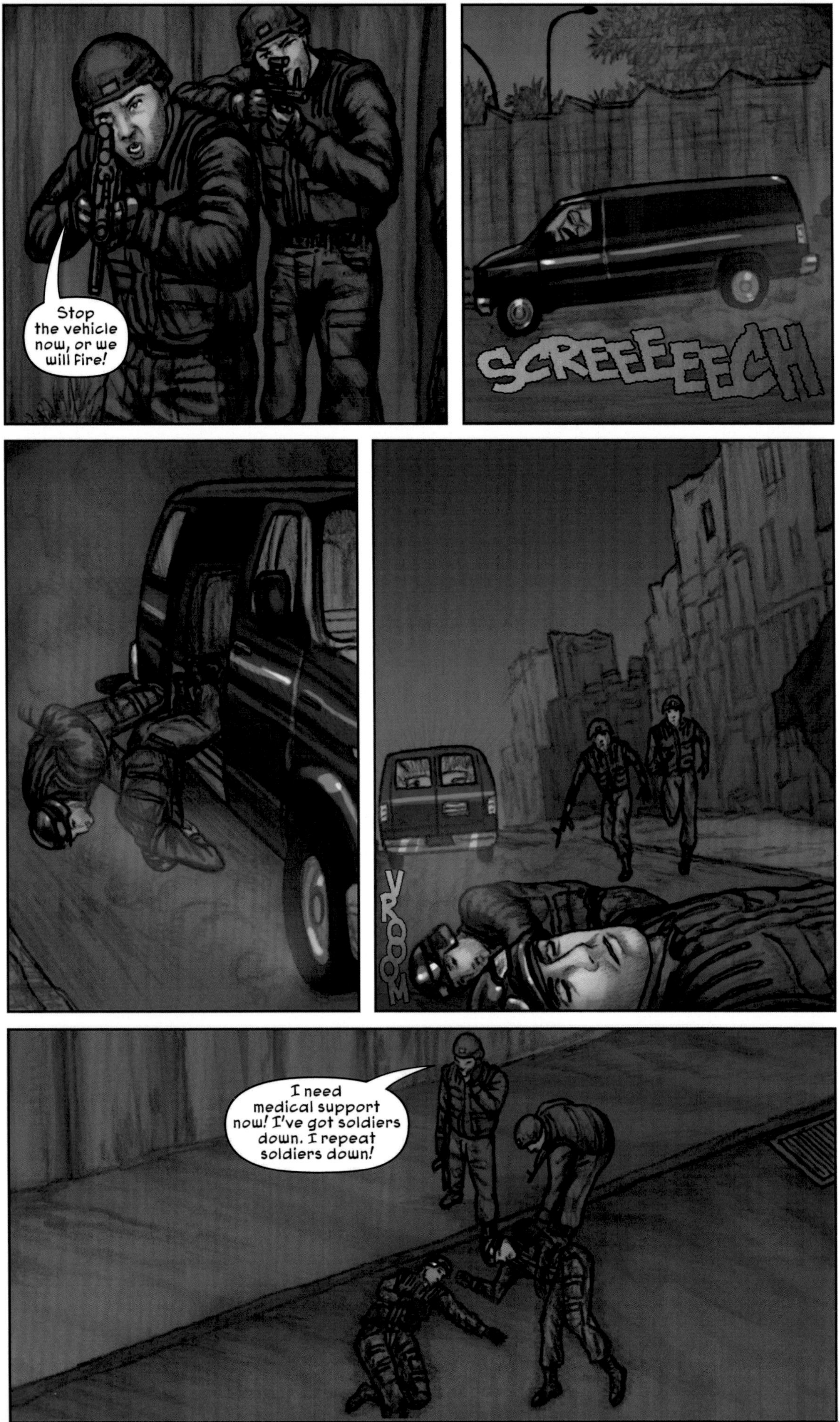
Stop the vehicle now, or we will fire!
SCREEEEECH
VROOOM
I need medical support now! I've got soldiers down. I repeat soldiers down!

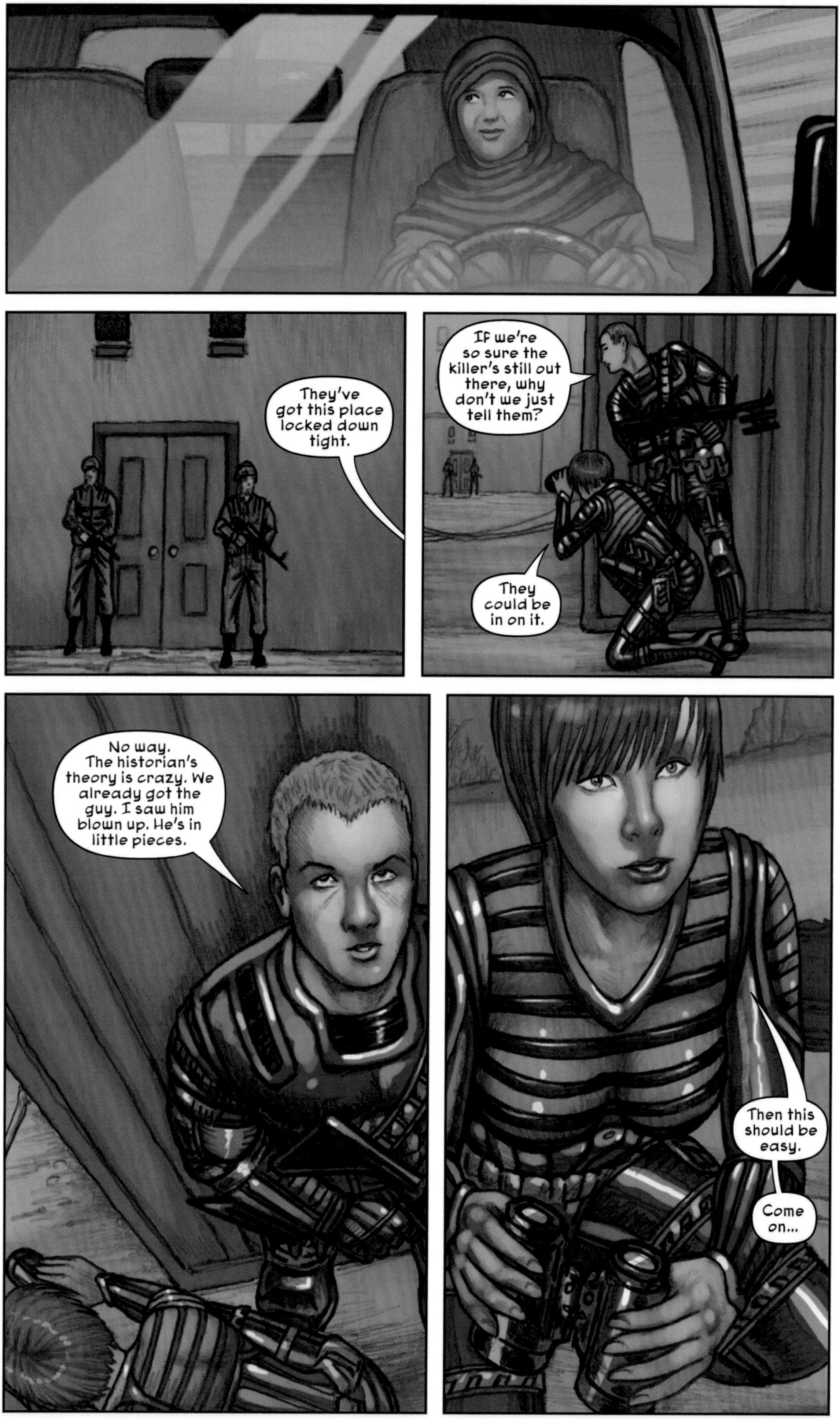
They've got this place locked down tight.
If we're so sure the killer's still out there, why don't we just tell them?
They could be in on it.
No way. The historian's theory is crazy. We already got the guy. I saw him blown up. He's in little pieces.
Then this should be easy.
Come on...

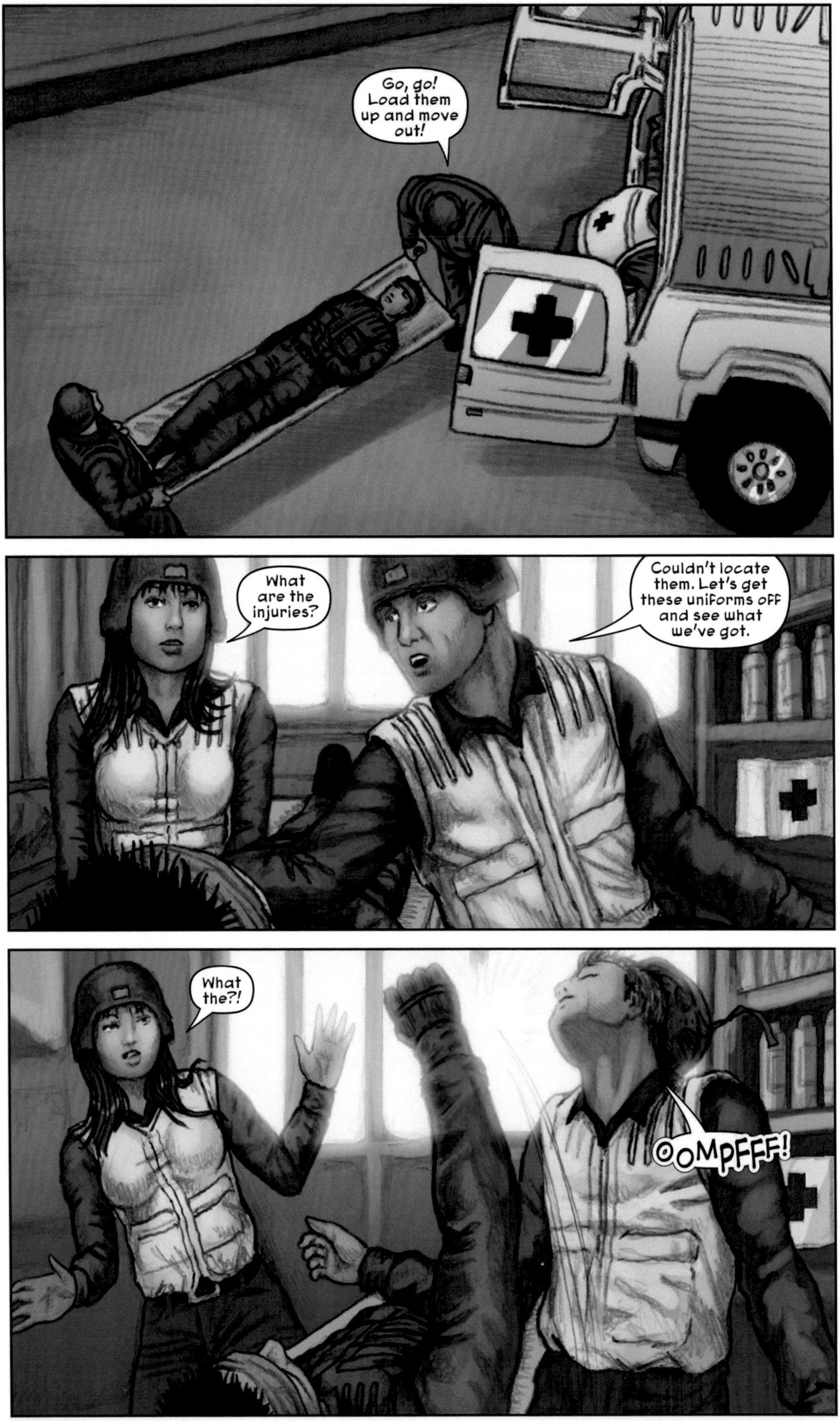
Go, go! Load them up and move out!
What are the injuries?
Couldn't locate them. Let's get these uniforms off and see what we've got.
What the?!
OOMPFFF!

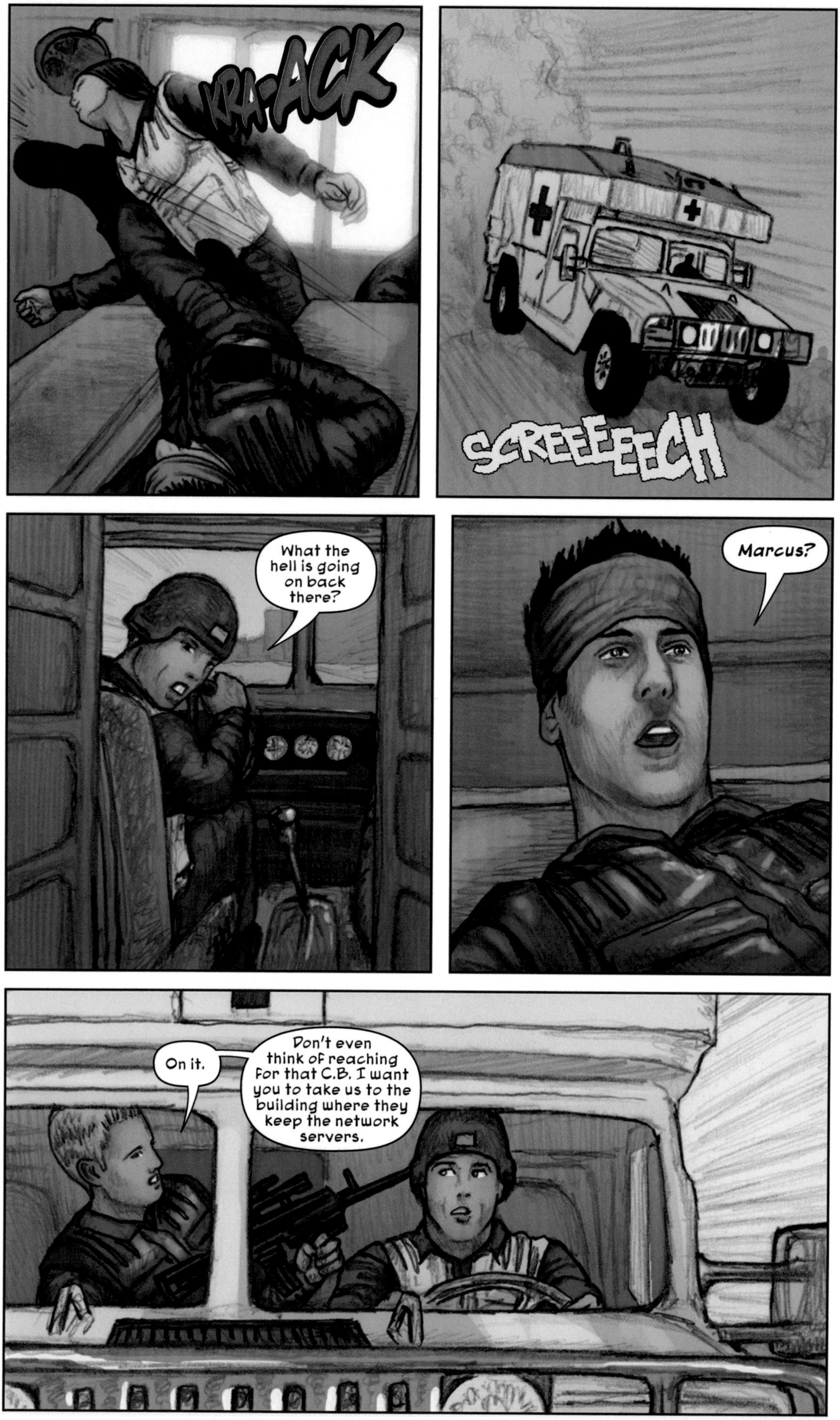
KRA-ACK
SCREEEEEECH
What the hell is going on back there?
Marcus?
On it.
Don't even think of reaching for that C.B. I want you to take us to the building where they keep the network servers.

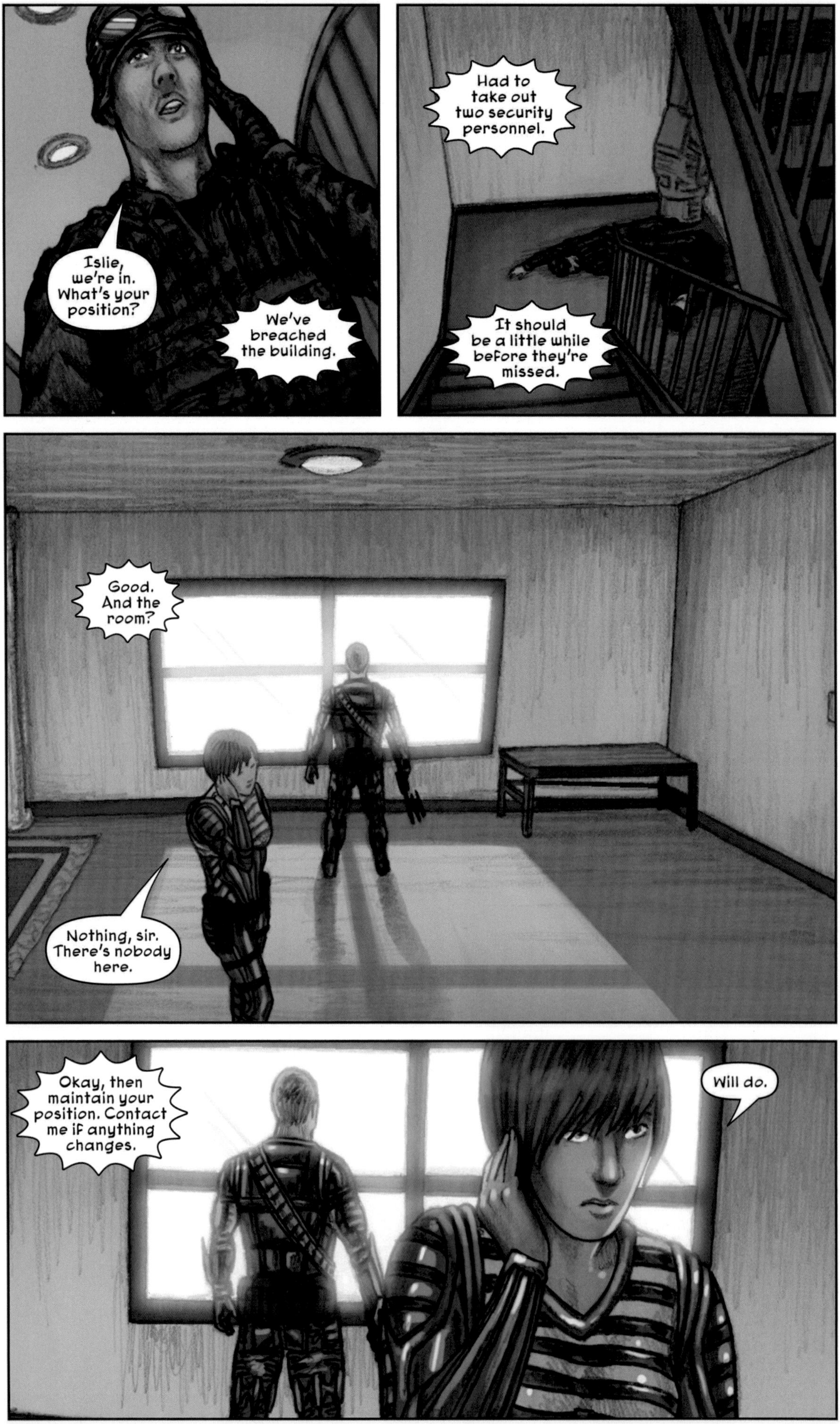

Islie, we're in. What's your position?
We've breached the building.
Had to take out two security personnel.
It should be a little while before they're missed.
Good. And the room?
Nothing, sir. There's nobody here.
Okay, then maintain your position. Contact me if anything changes.
Will do.

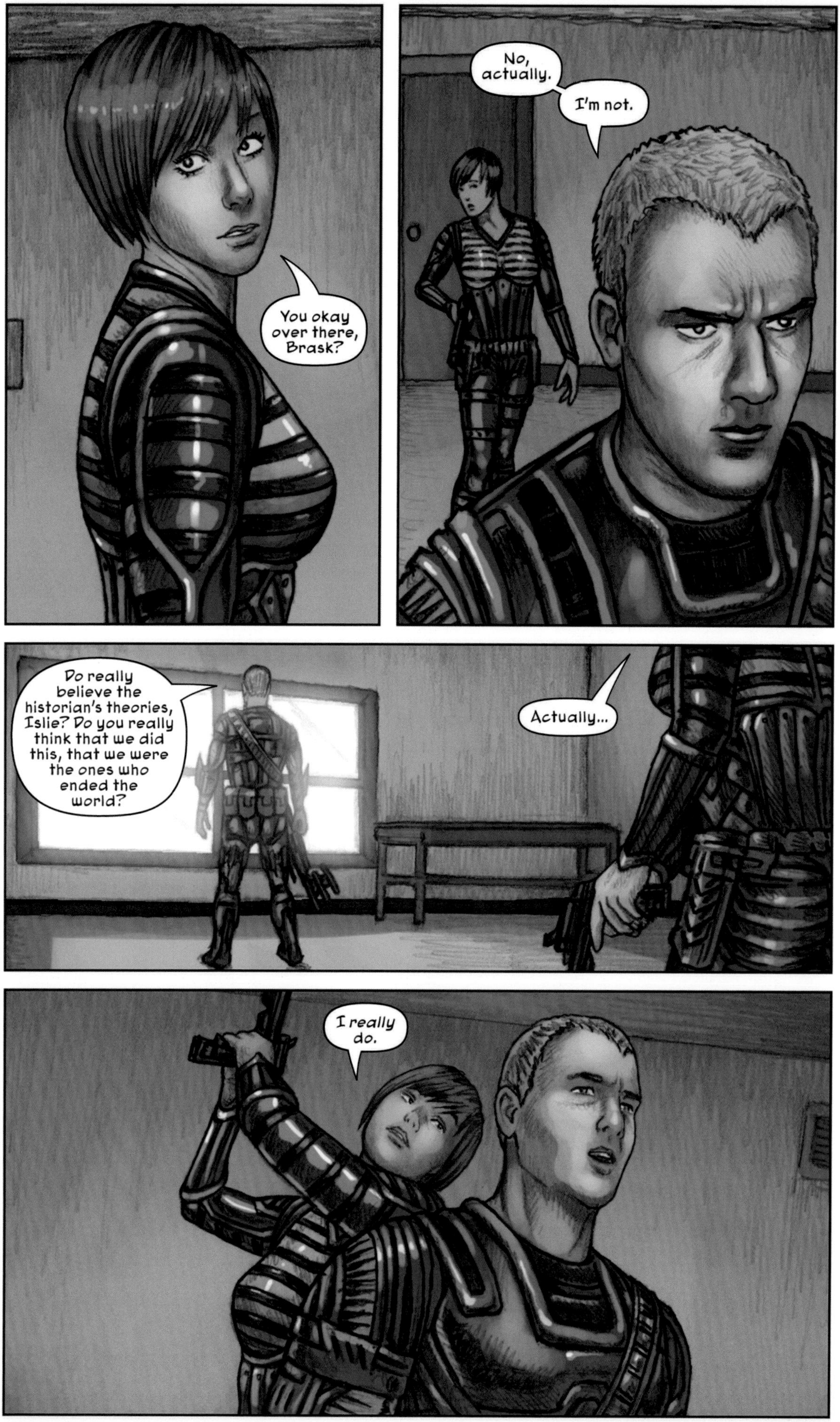
You okay over there, Brask?
No, actually.
I'm not.
Do really believe the historian's theories, Islie? Do you really think that we did this, that we were the ones who ended the world?
Actually...
I really do.

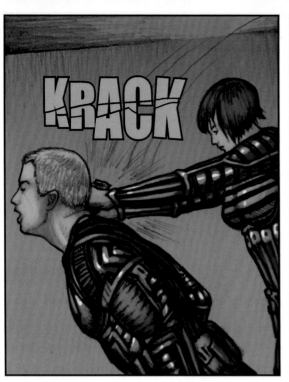

KRACK

What are you... why?

Did you think there weren't people who already knew the truth, Brask? That everybody was as ignorant as the historian?

No, people knew.

CRRUSSH

Those same people think that we shouldn't be allowed to mess with history. They think humanity should have to live with its mistakes.

You're insane.
I'm insane? Have you looked at yourself recently? You're falling apart.
But don't worry, it'll all be over soon.
It's time to take your pills.
Don't feel bad, Brask. There's nothing you could have done.
It's history.
All of this has already happened.

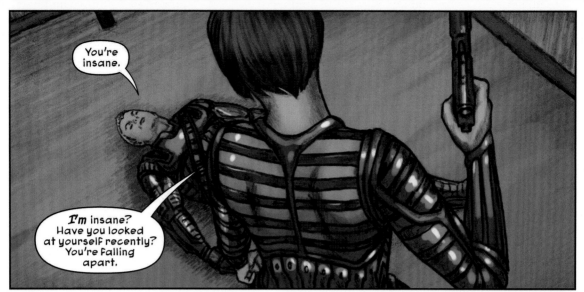

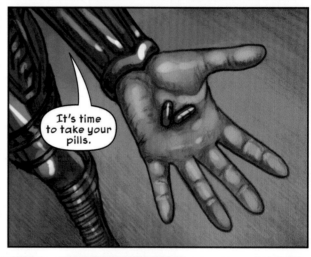

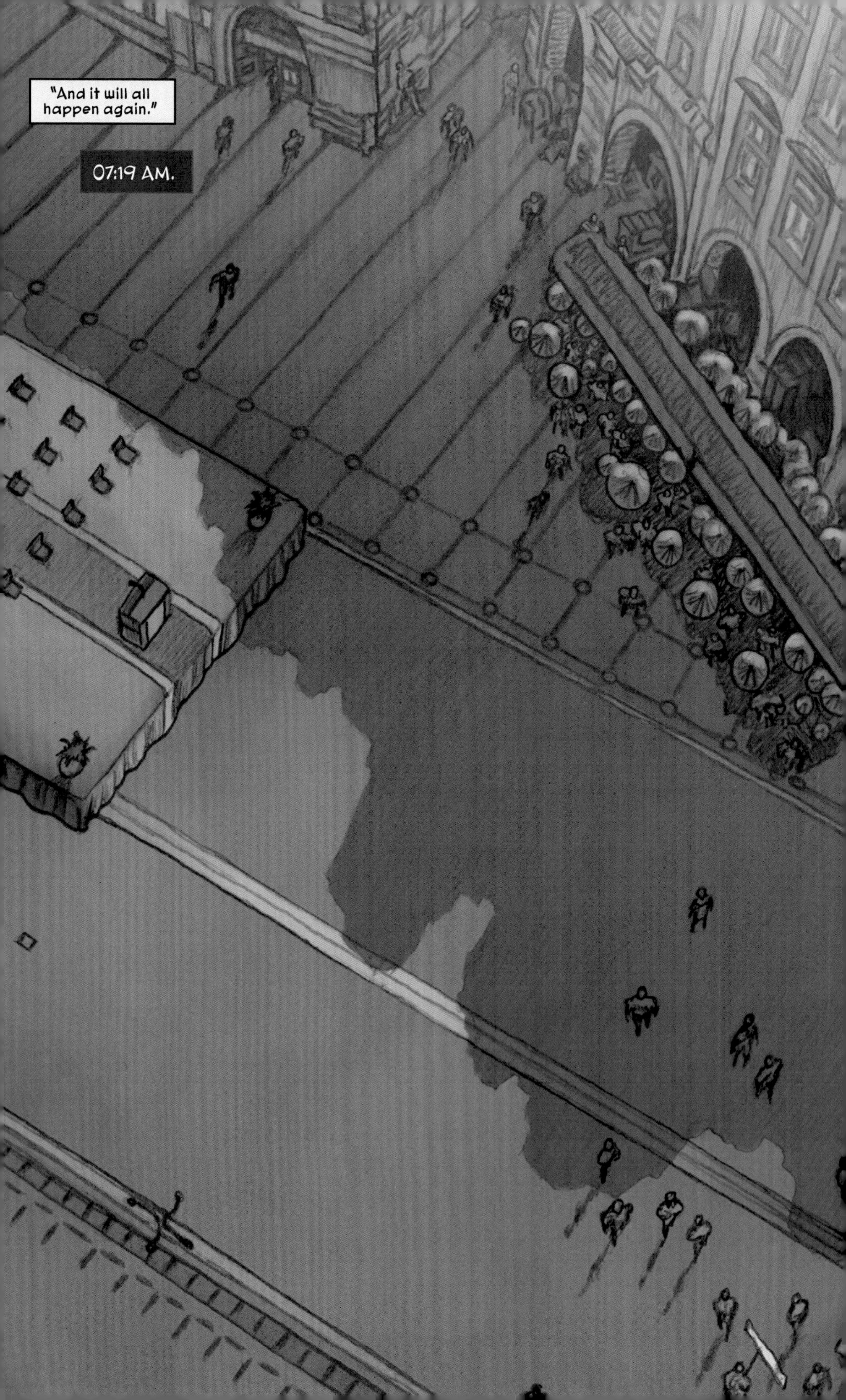
"And it will all happen again."
07:19 AM.

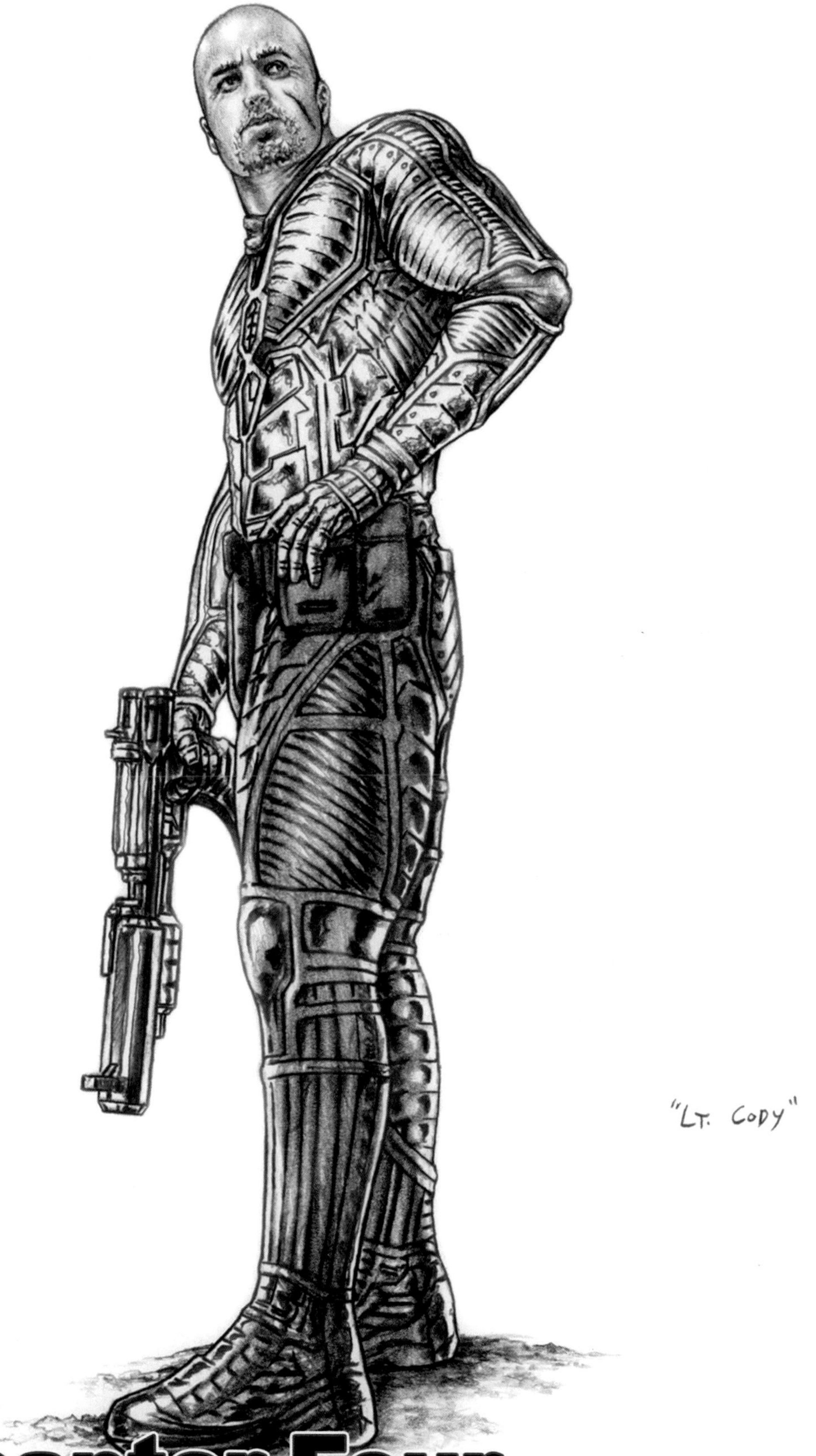
"LT. CODY"

Chapter Four

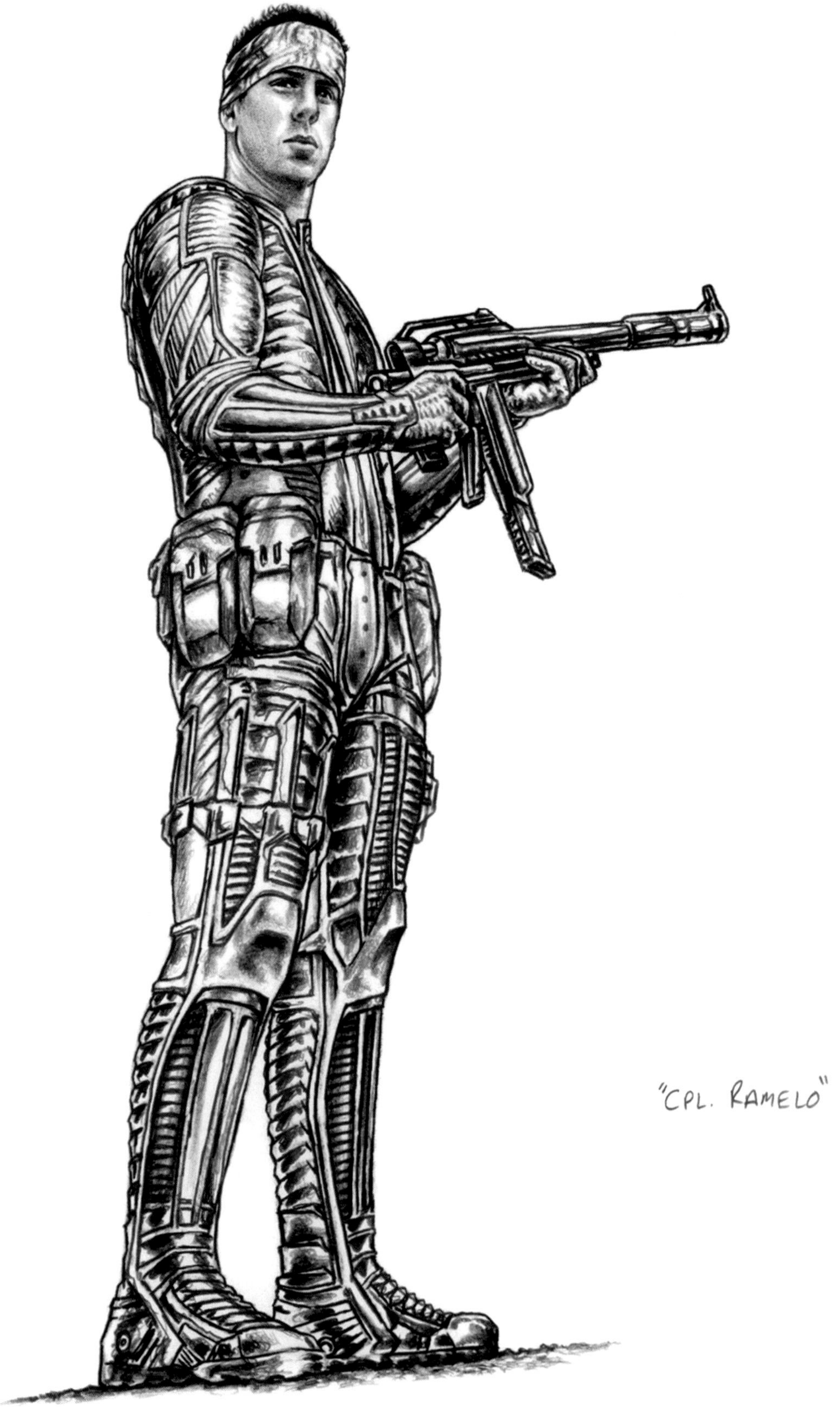
"CPL. RAMELO"

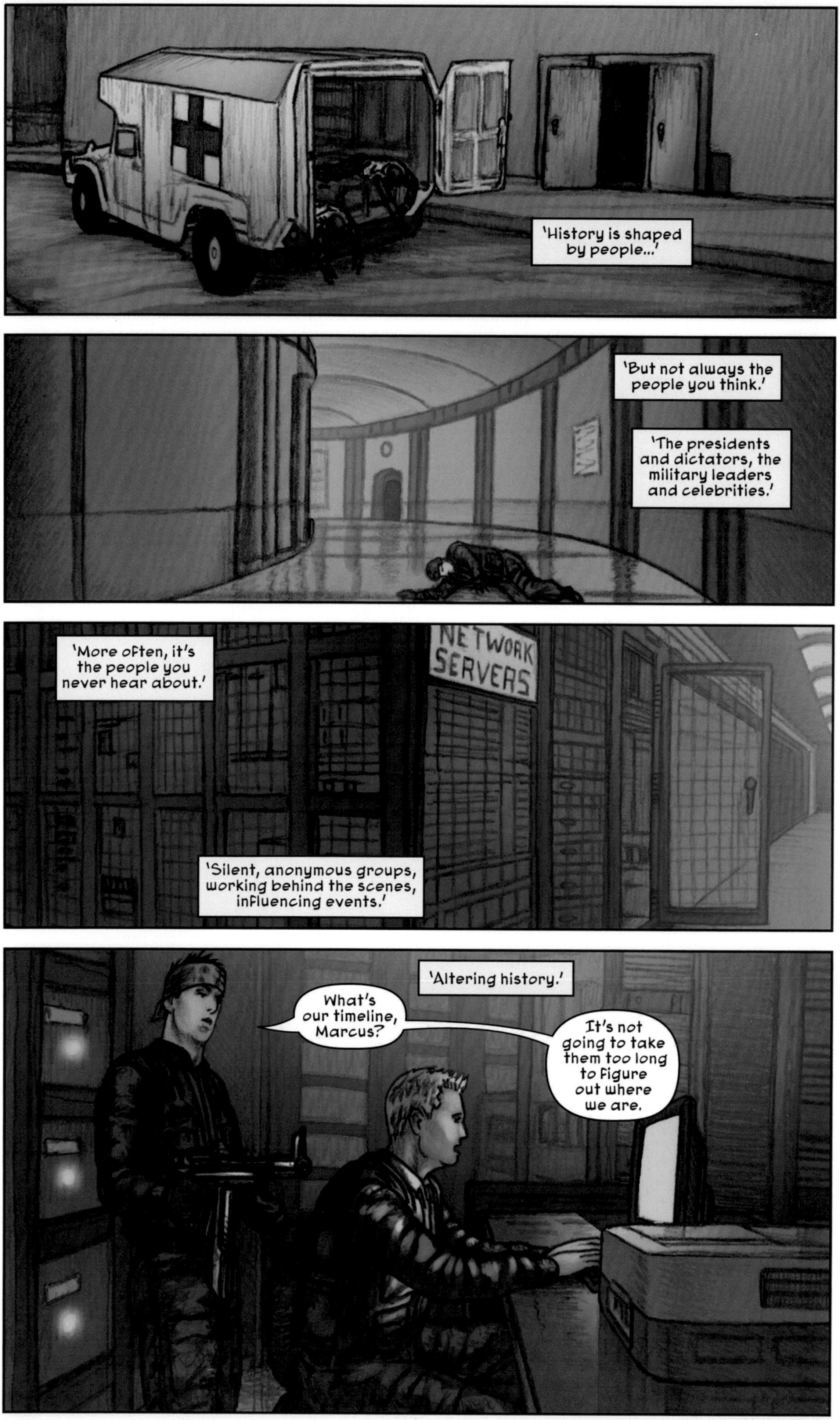
'History is shaped by people...'
'But not always the people you think.'
'The presidents and dictators, the military leaders and celebrities.'
NETWORK SERVERS
'More often, it's the people you never hear about.'
'Silent, anonymous groups, working behind the scenes, influencing events.'
'Altering history.'
What's our timeline, Marcus?
It's not going to take them too long to figure out where we are.

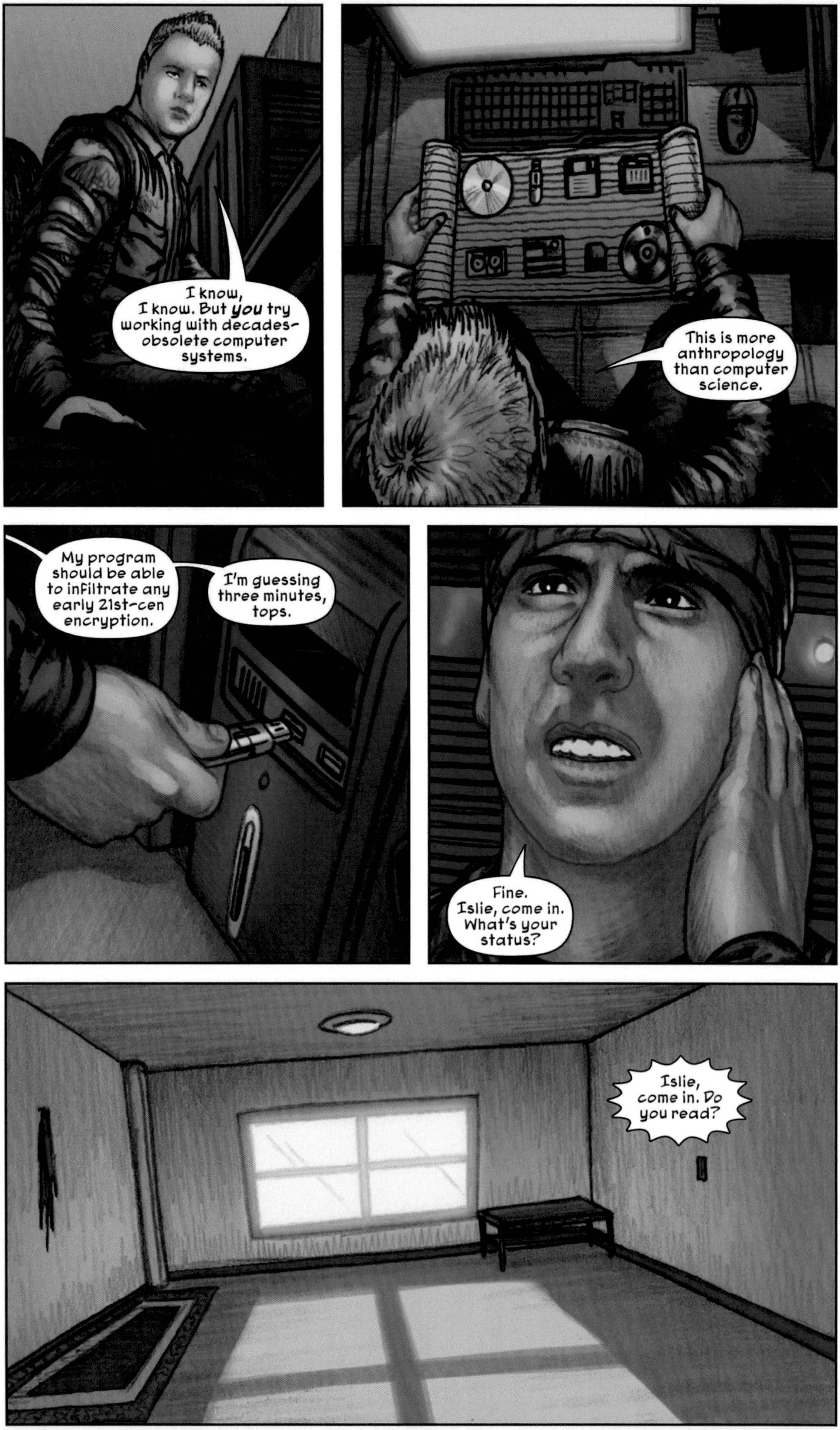
I know, I know. But *you* try working with decades-obsolete computer systems.
This is more anthropology than computer science.
My program should be able to infiltrate any early 21st-cen encryption.
I'm guessing three minutes, tops.
Fine. Islie, come in. What's your status?
Islie, come in. Do you read?

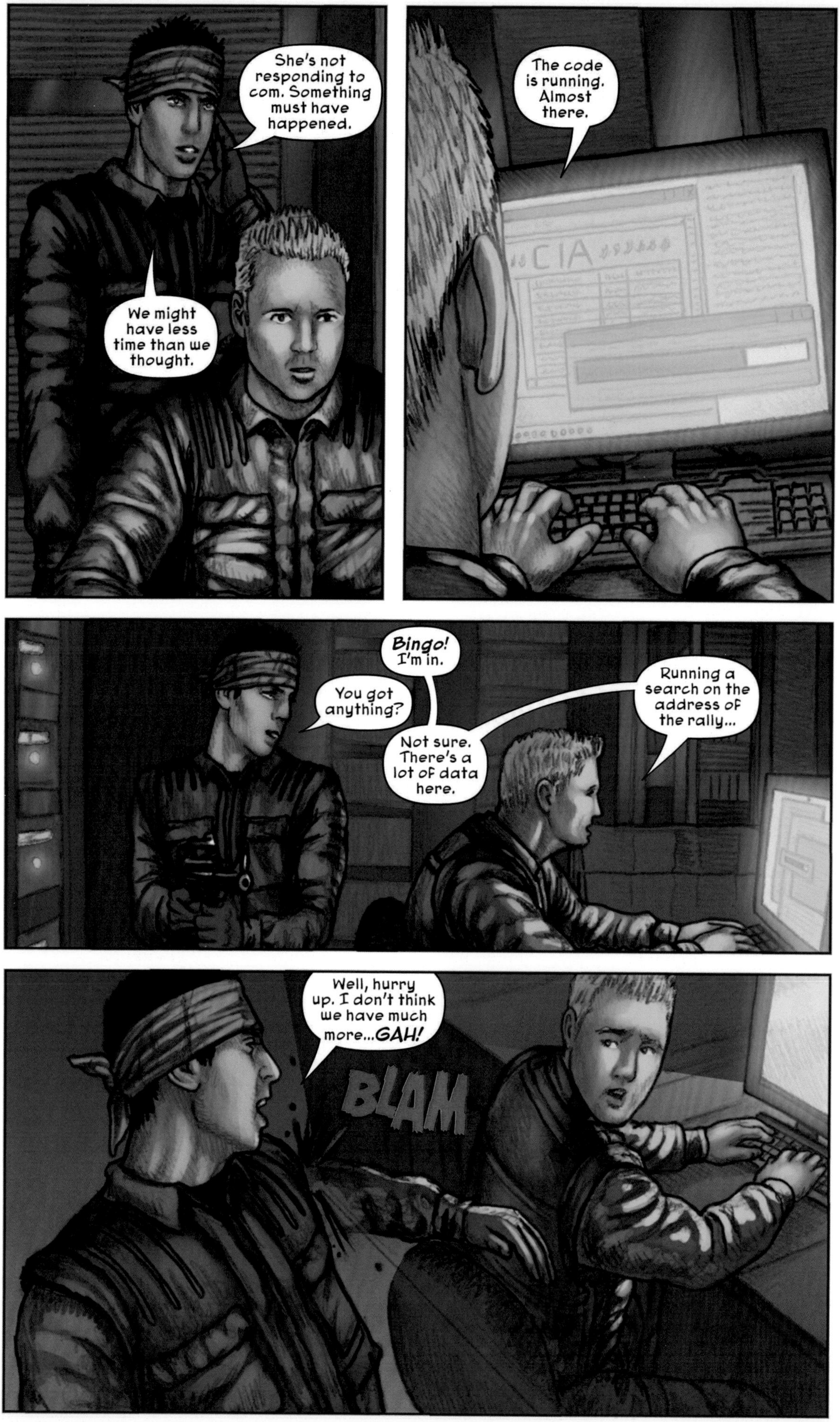
She's not responding to com. Something must have happened.
We might have less time than we thought.
The code is running. Almost there.
CIA
Bingo! I'm in.
You got anything?
Not sure. There's a lot of data here.
Running a search on the address of the rally...
Well, hurry up. I don't think we have much more...*GAH!*
BLAM

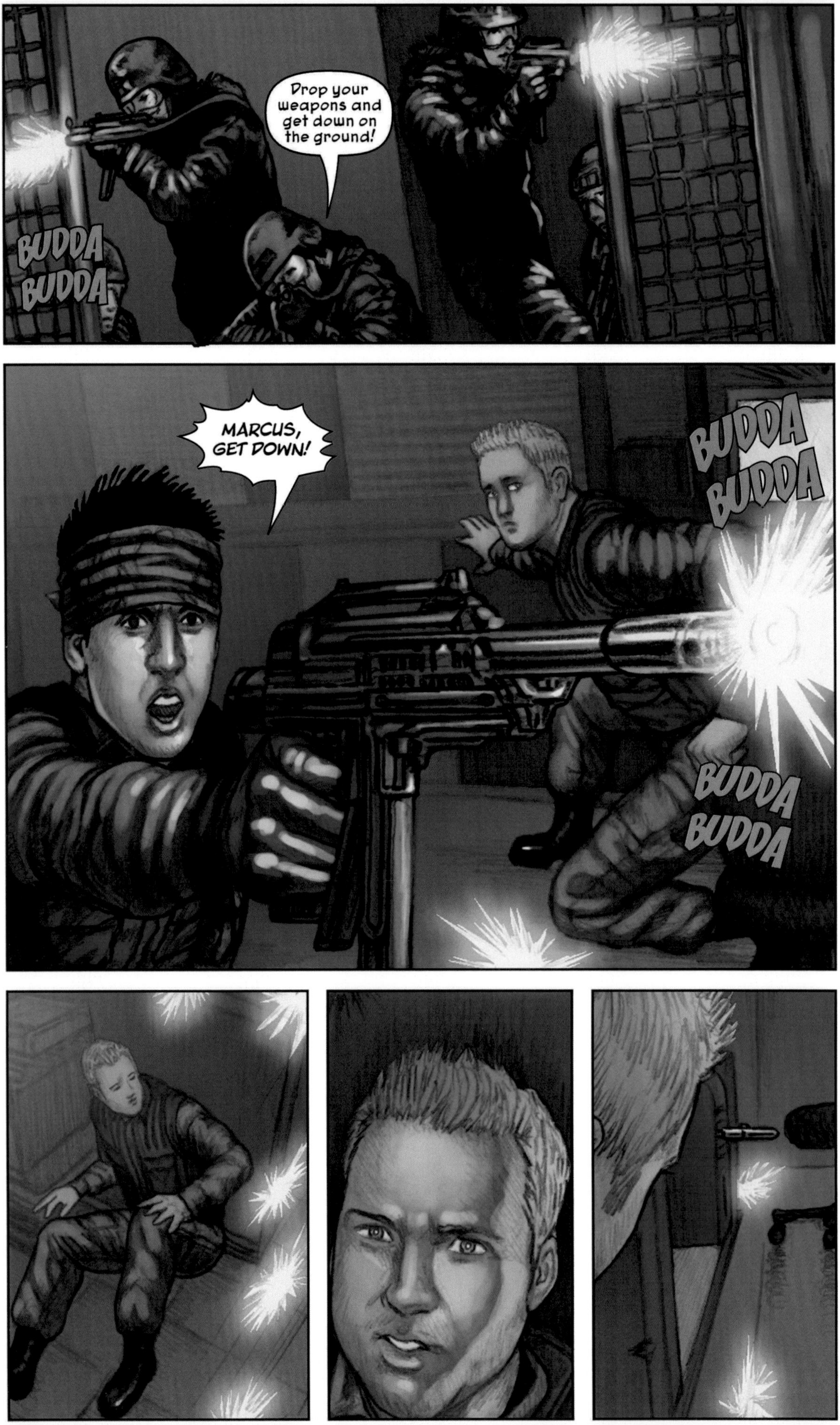
Drop your weapons and get down on the ground!
BUDDA BUDDA
MARCUS, GET DOWN!
BUDDA BUDDA
BUDDA BUDDA

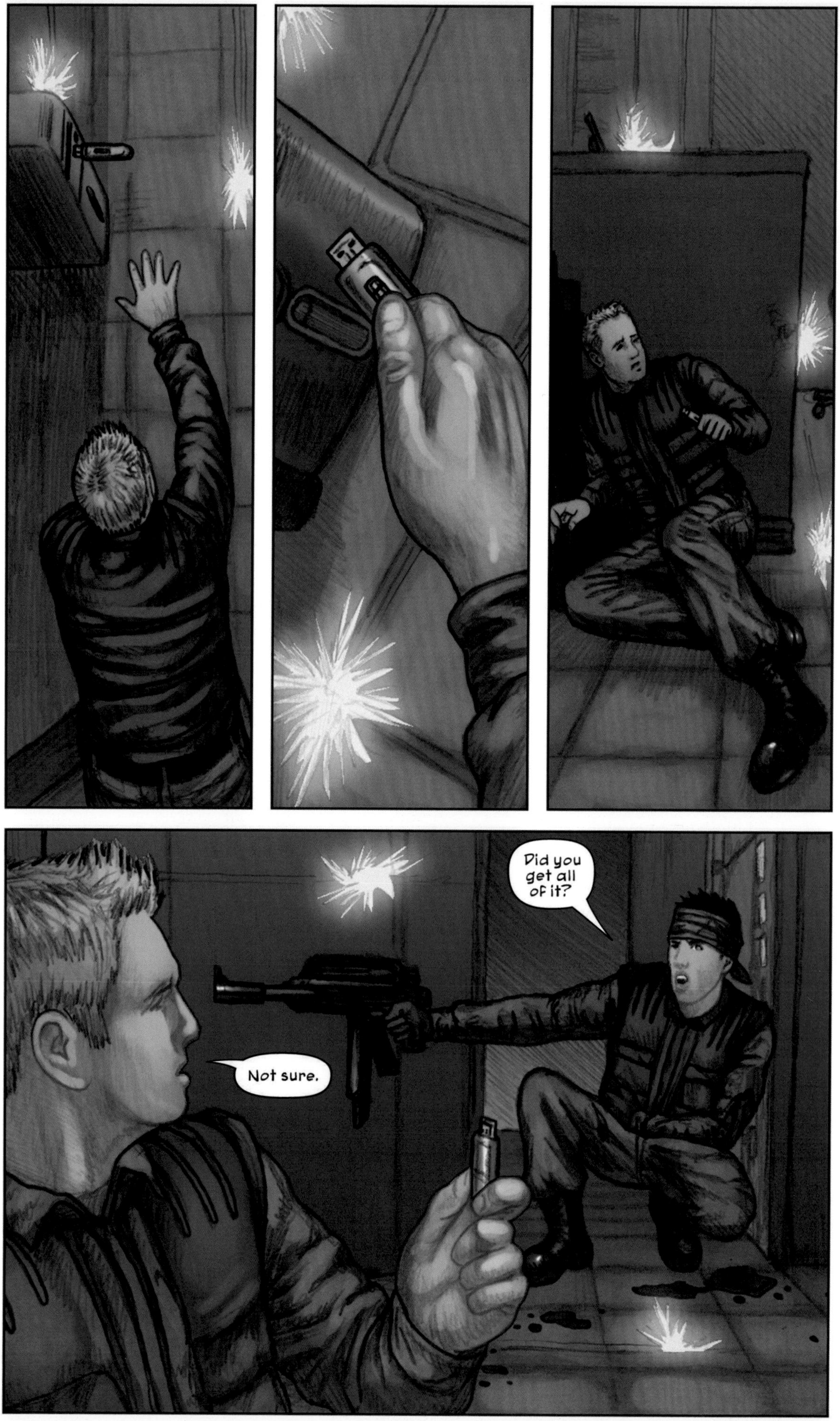
Did you get all of it?
Not sure.

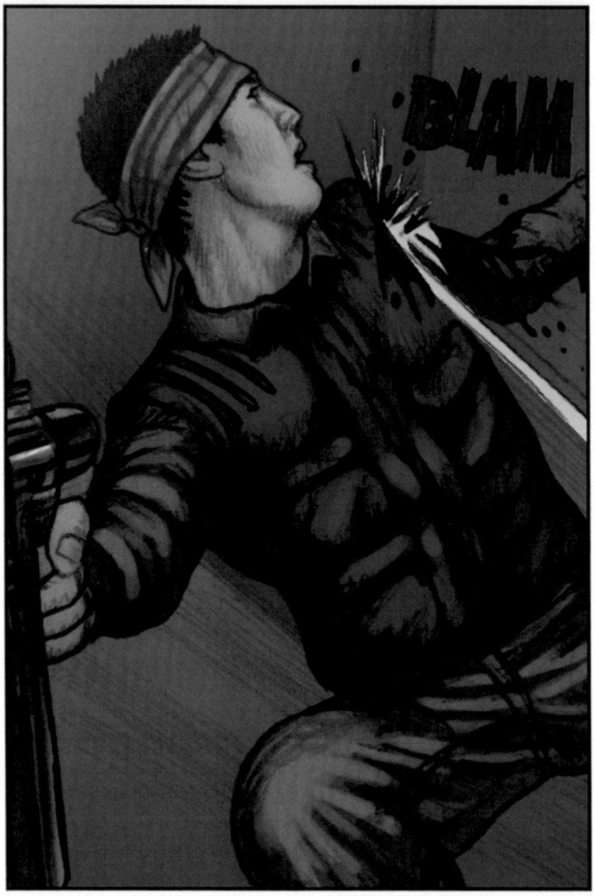
BLAM

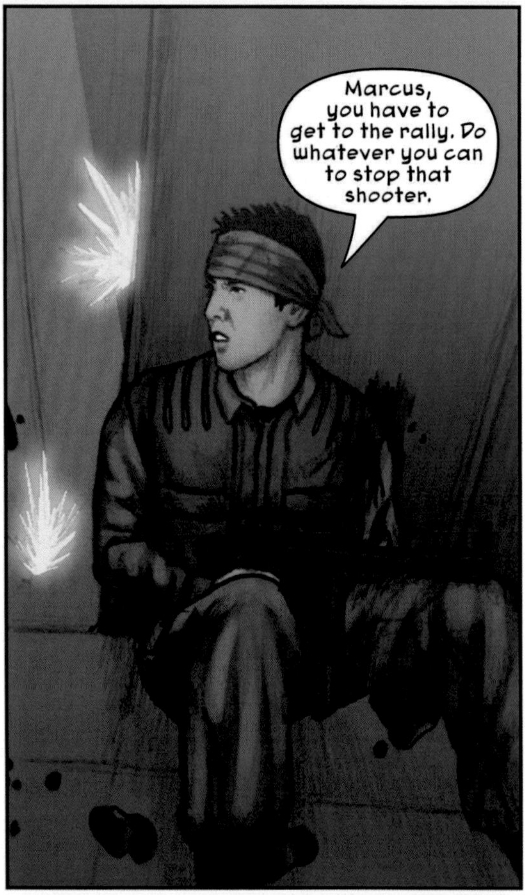
Marcus, you have to get to the rally. Do whatever you can to stop that shooter.

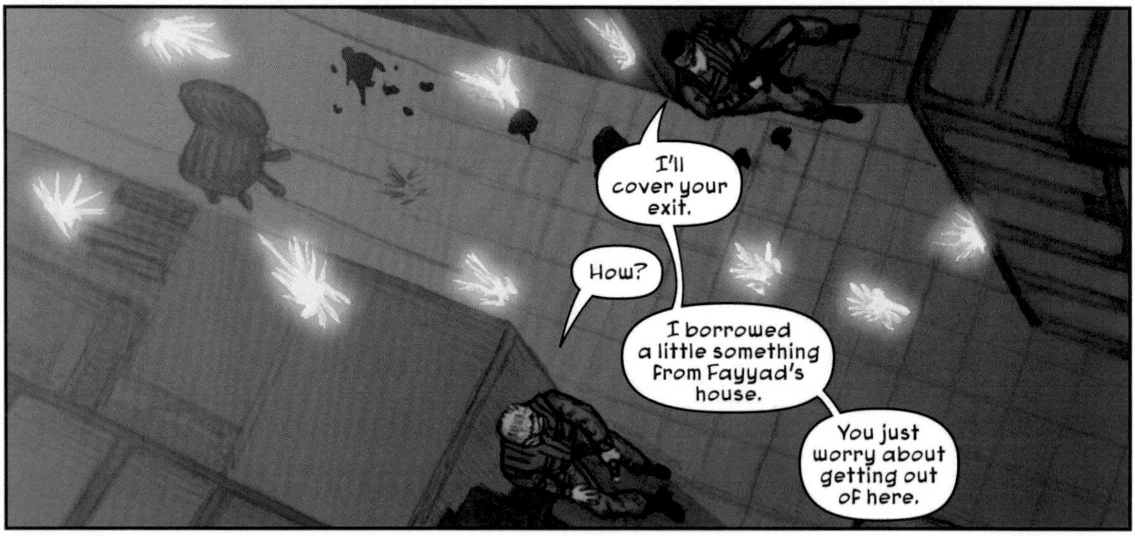
I'll cover your exit.
How?
I borrowed a little something from Fayyad's house.
You just worry about getting out of here.

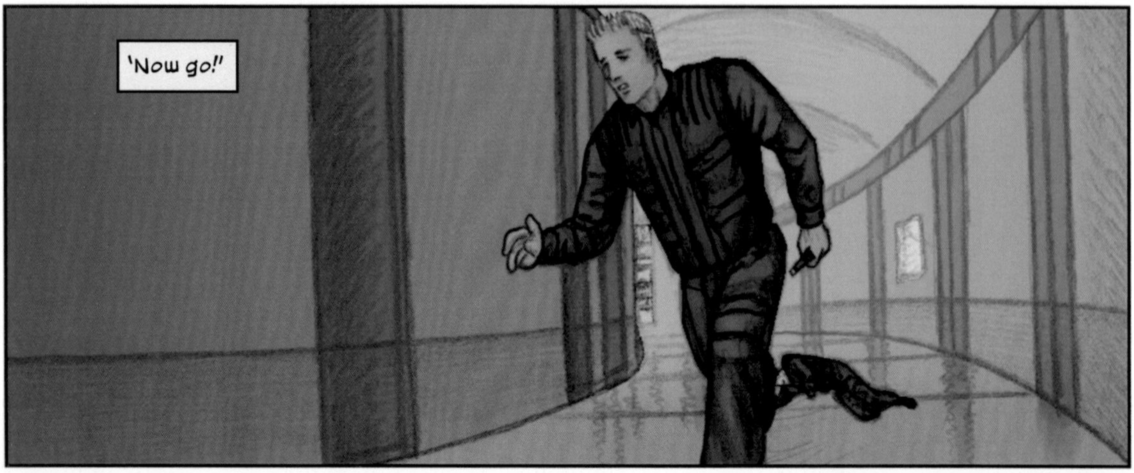
'Now go!'

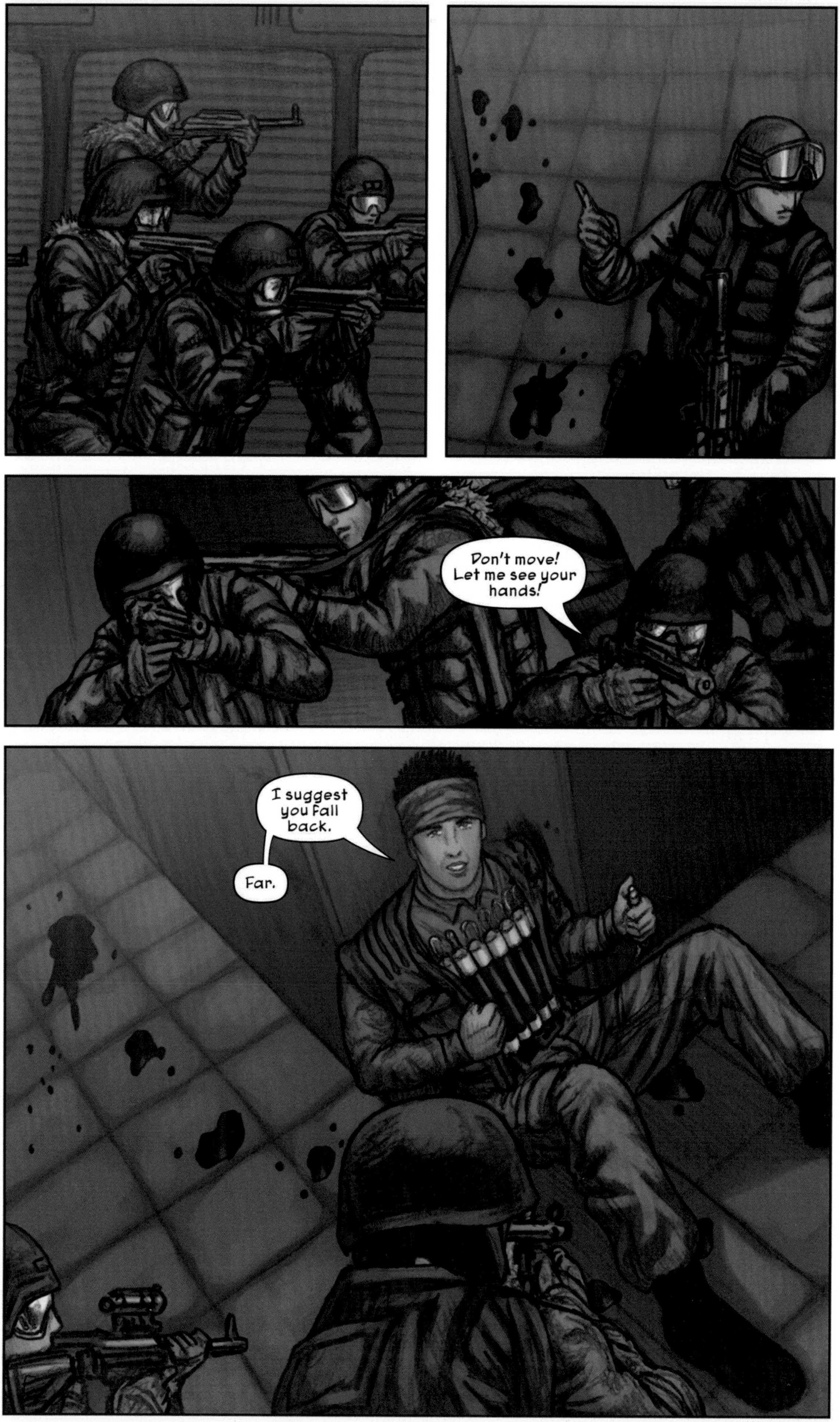
Don't move! Let me see your hands!
I suggest you fall back.
Far.

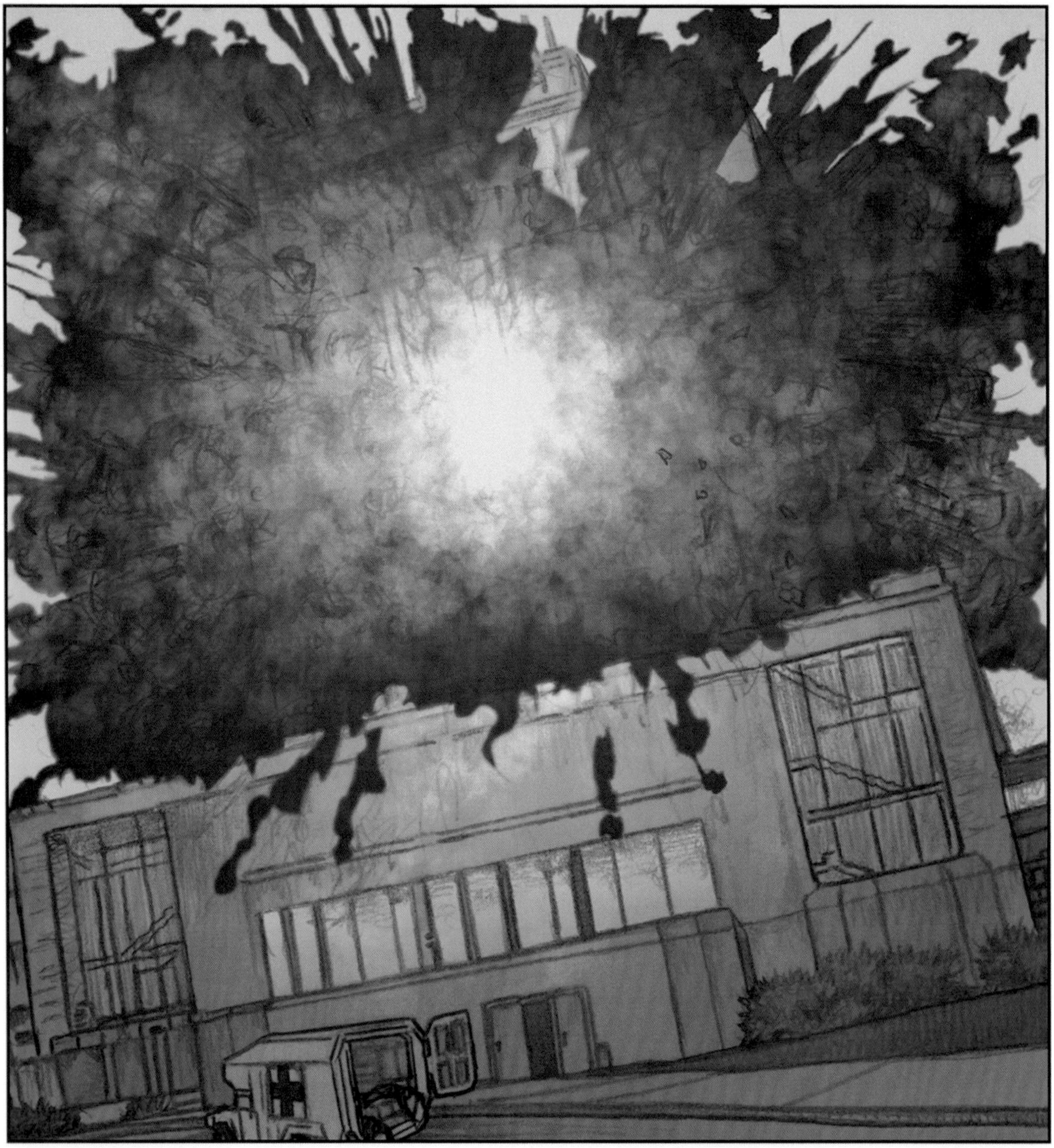

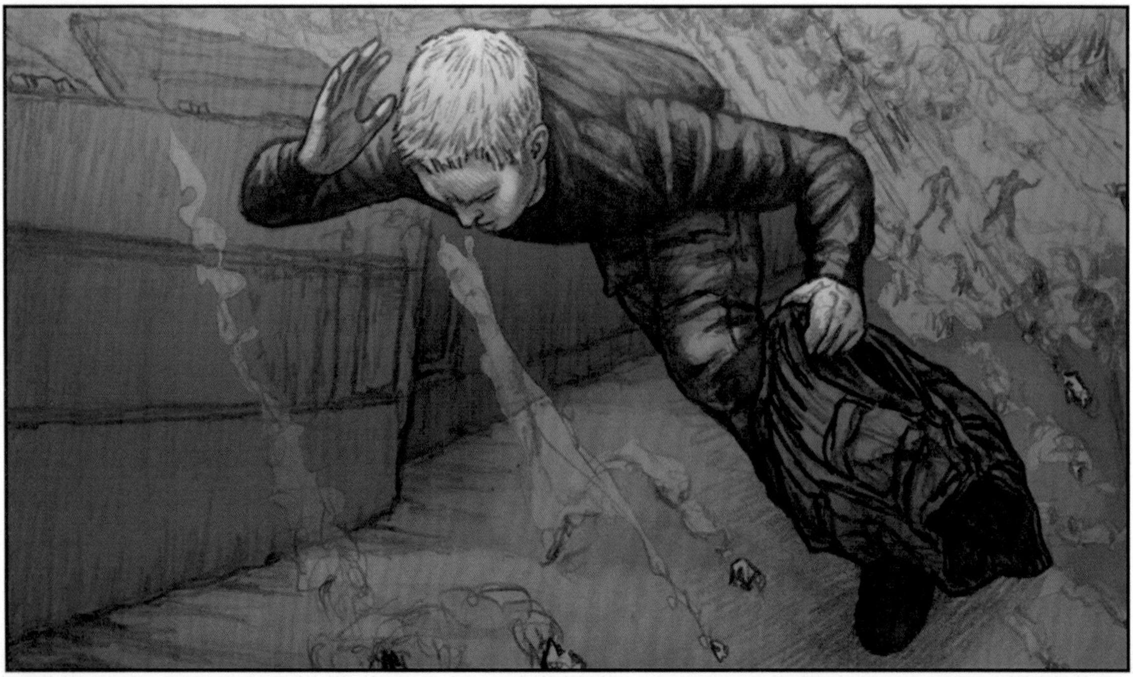

Aarya, come to the south-east corner. I'll meet you on the street.

We've lost contact with Islie and Brask.

We need to get to that rally.

Where is your friend Ramelo?

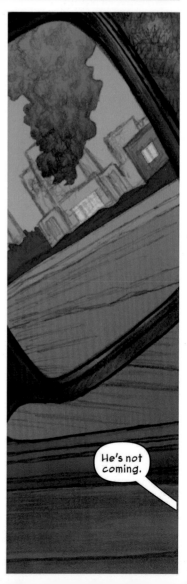

He's not coming.

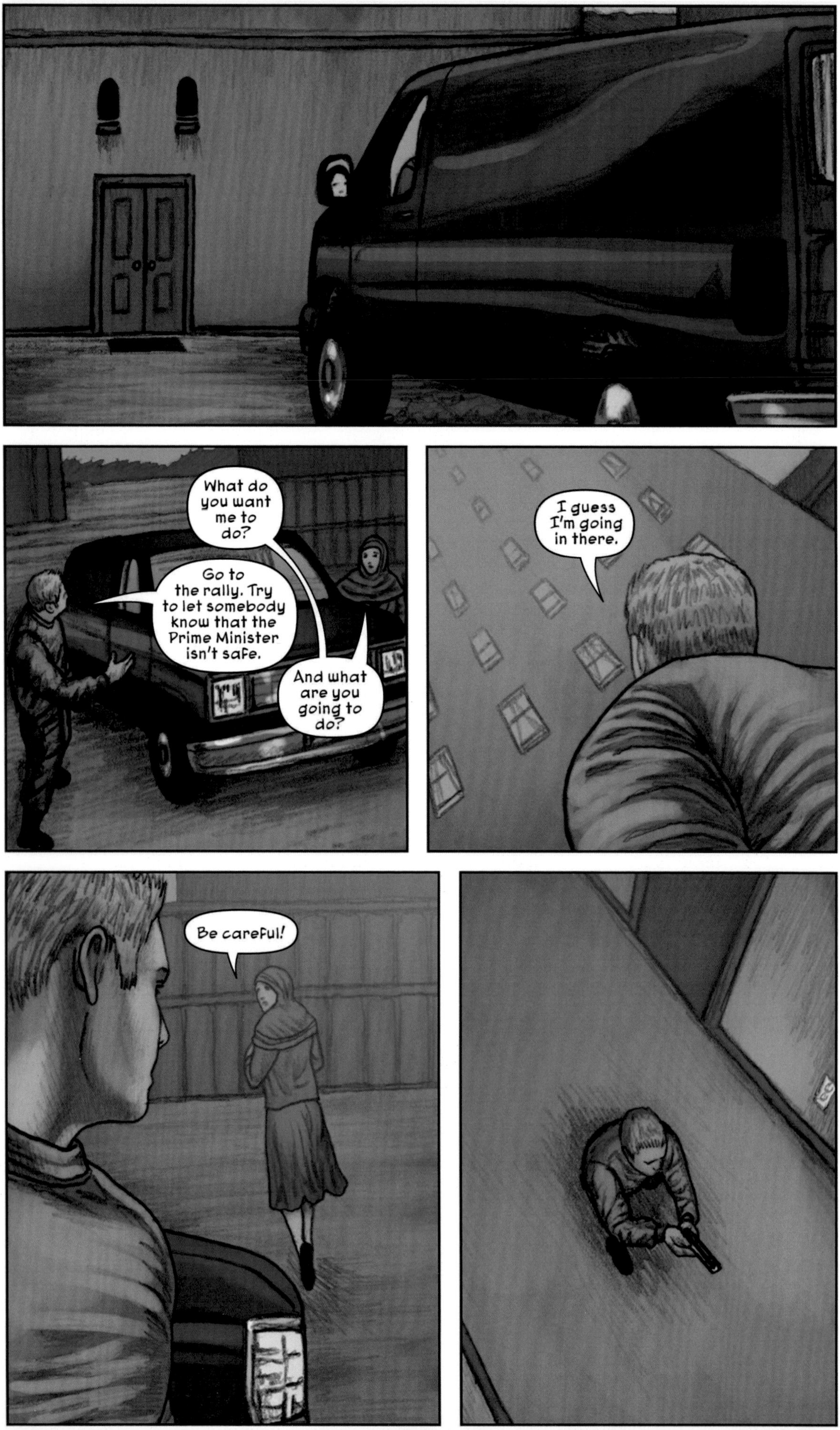
What do you want me to do?
Go to the rally. Try to let somebody know that the Prime Minister isn't safe.
And what are you going to do?
I guess I'm going in there.
Be careful!

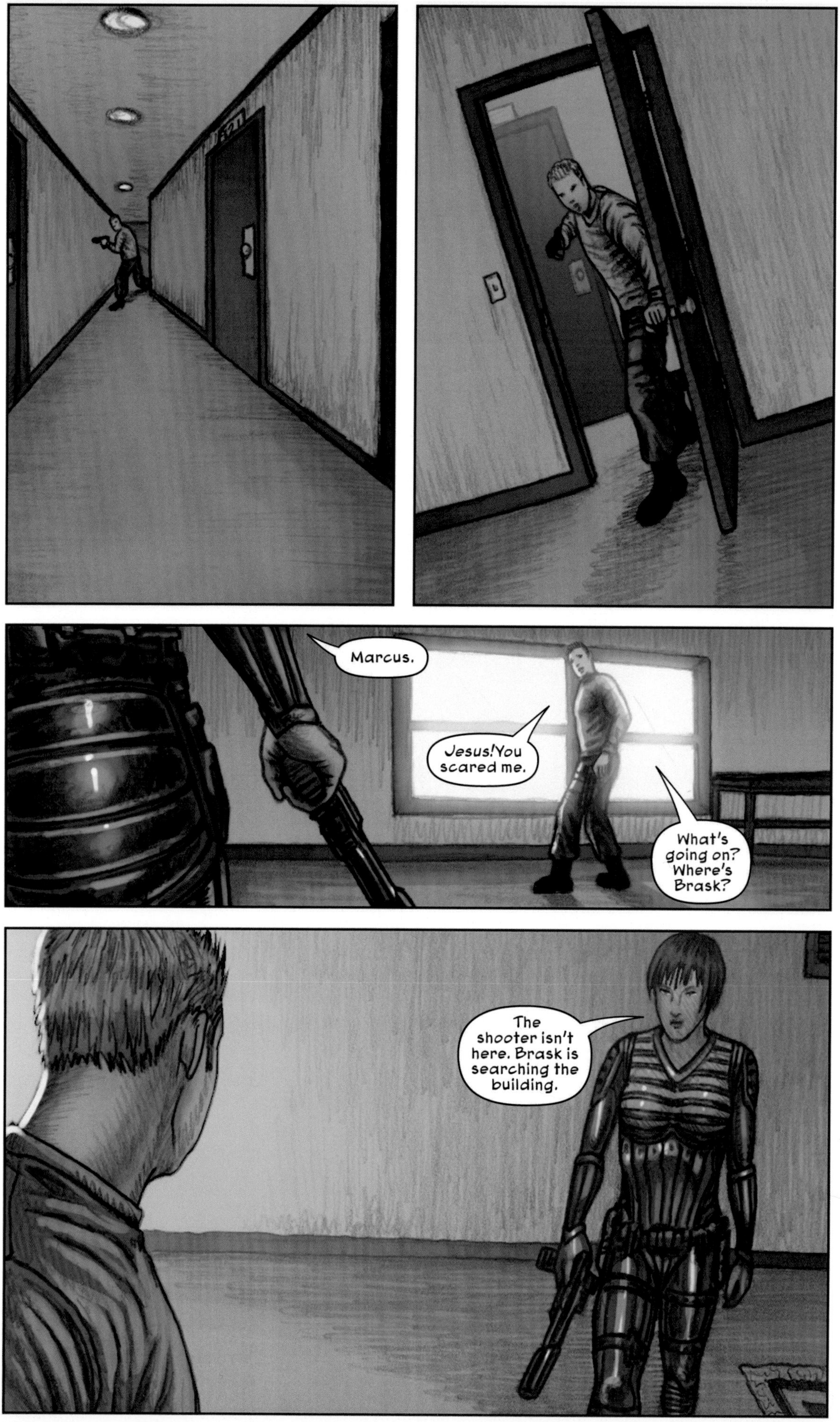
Marcus.
Jesus! You scared me.
What's going on? Where's Brask?
The shooter isn't here. Brask is searching the building.

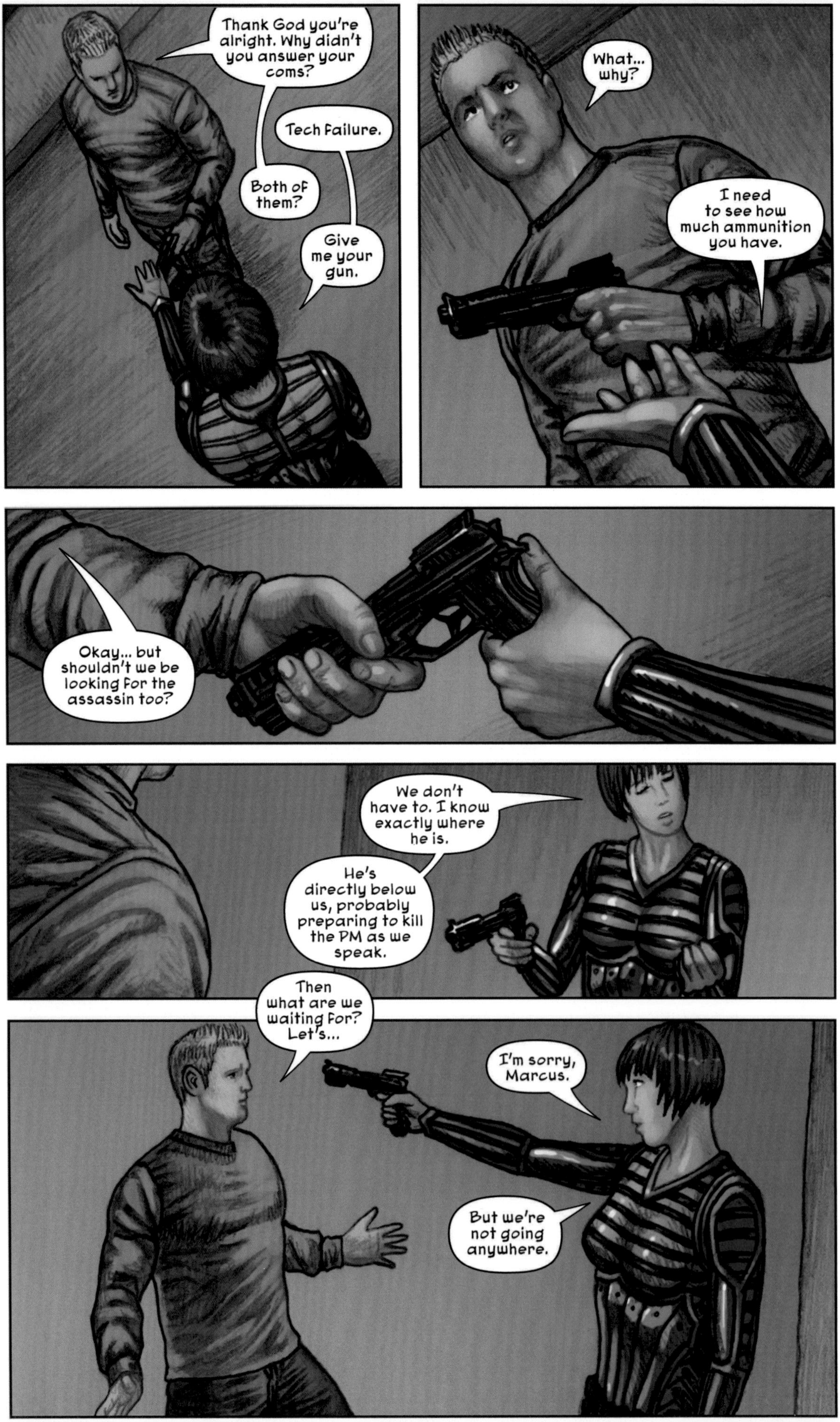
Thank God you're alright. Why didn't you answer your coms?
Tech failure.
Both of them?
Give me your gun.
What... why?
I need to see how much ammunition you have.
Okay... but shouldn't we be looking for the assassin too?
We don't have to. I know exactly where he is.
He's directly below us, probably preparing to kill the PM as we speak.
Then what are we waiting for? Let's...
I'm sorry, Marcus.
But we're not going anywhere.

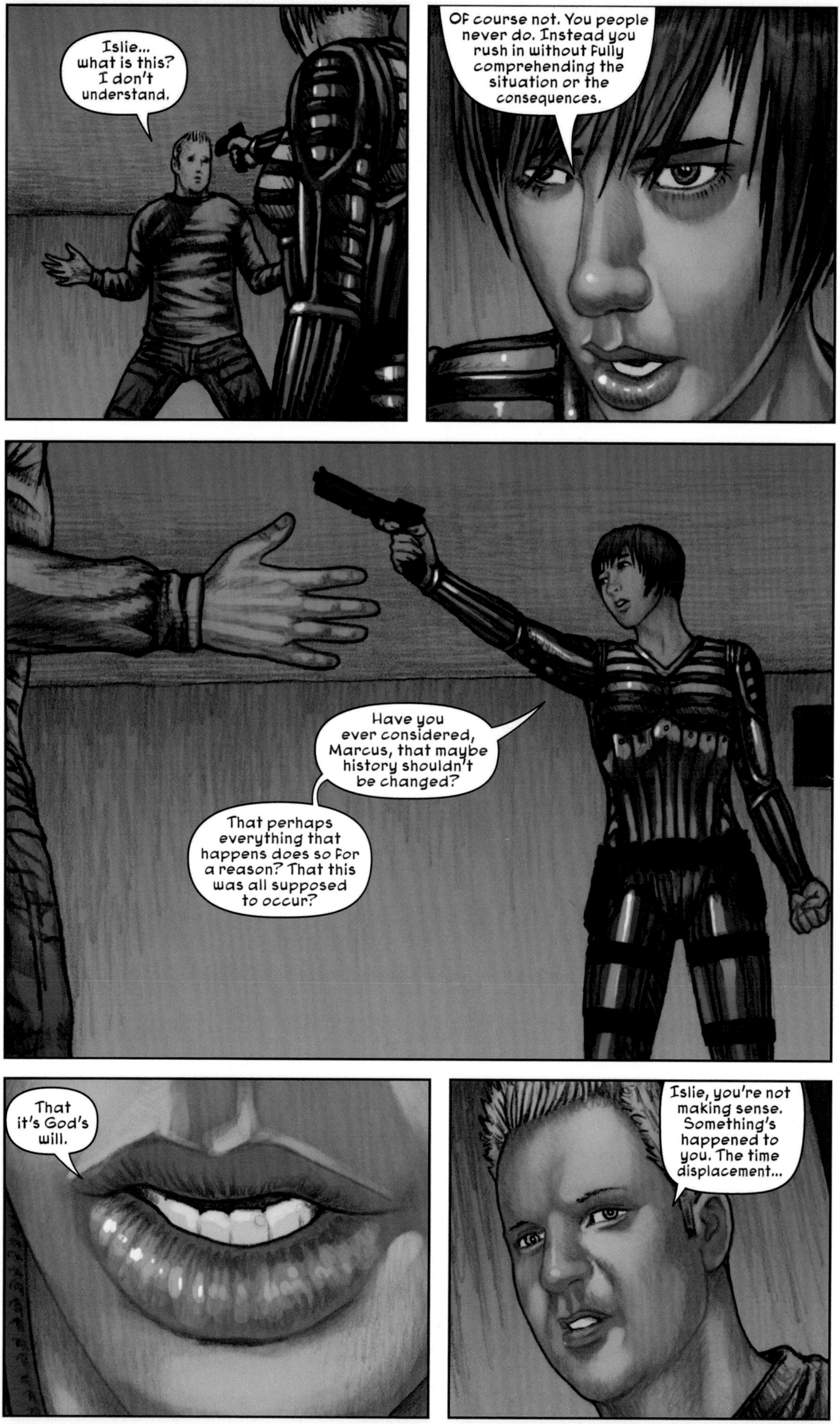
Islie... what is this? I don't understand.
Of course not. You people never do. Instead you rush in without fully comprehending the situation or the consequences.
Have you ever considered, Marcus, that maybe history shouldn't be changed?
That perhaps everything that happens does so for a reason? That this was all supposed to occur?
That it's God's will.
Islie, you're not making sense. Something's happened to you. The time displacement...

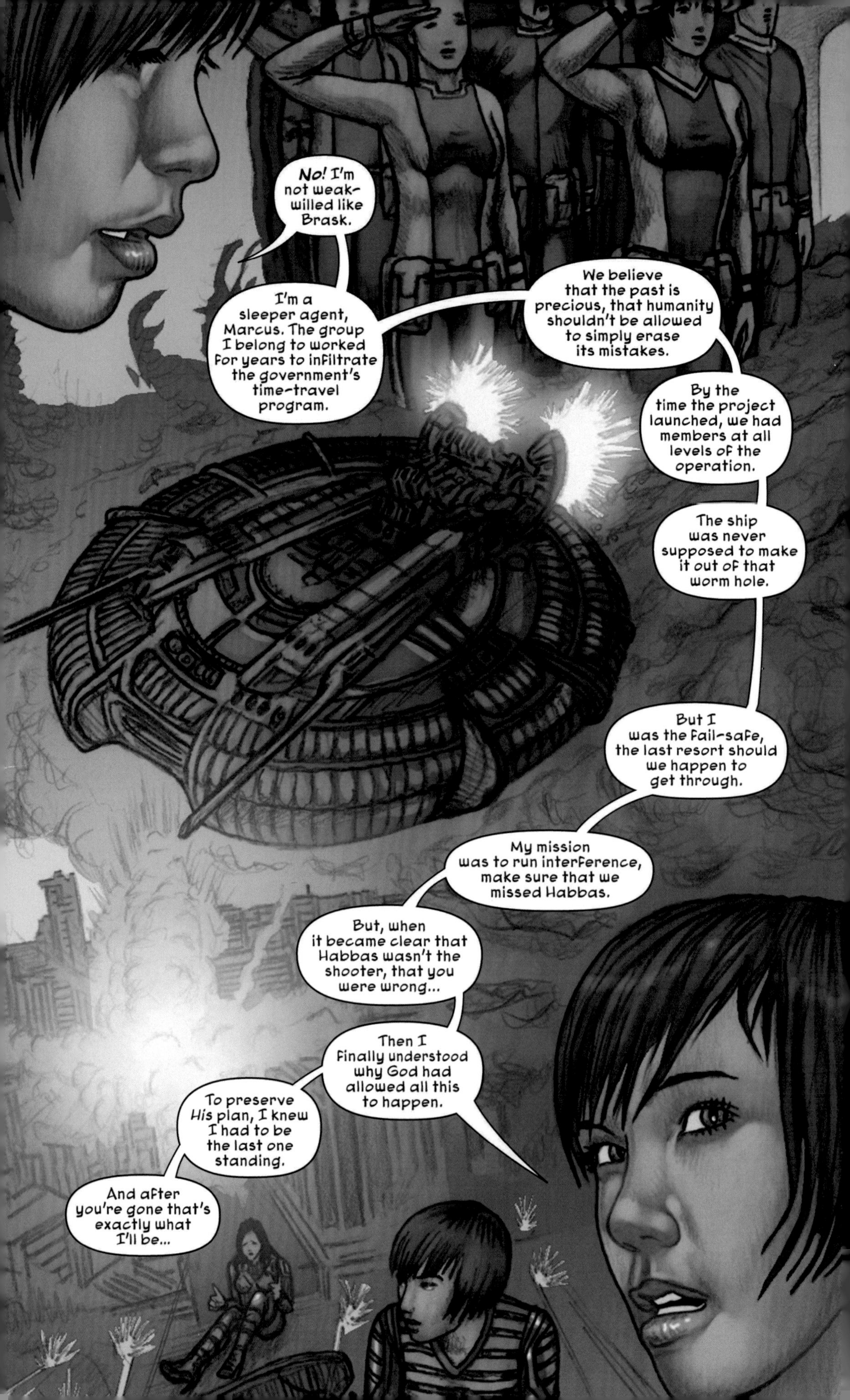

No! I'm not weak-willed like Brask.
I'm a sleeper agent, Marcus. The group I belong to worked for years to infiltrate the government's time-travel program.
We believe that the past is precious, that humanity shouldn't be allowed to simply erase its mistakes.
By the time the project launched, we had members at all levels of the operation.
The ship was never supposed to make it out of that worm hole.
But I was the fail-safe, the last resort should we happen to get through.
My mission was to run interference, make sure that we missed Habbas.
But, when it became clear that Habbas wasn't the shooter, that you were wrong...
Then I finally understood why God had allowed all this to happen.
To preserve His plan, I knew I had to be the last one standing.
And after you're gone that's exactly what I'll be...

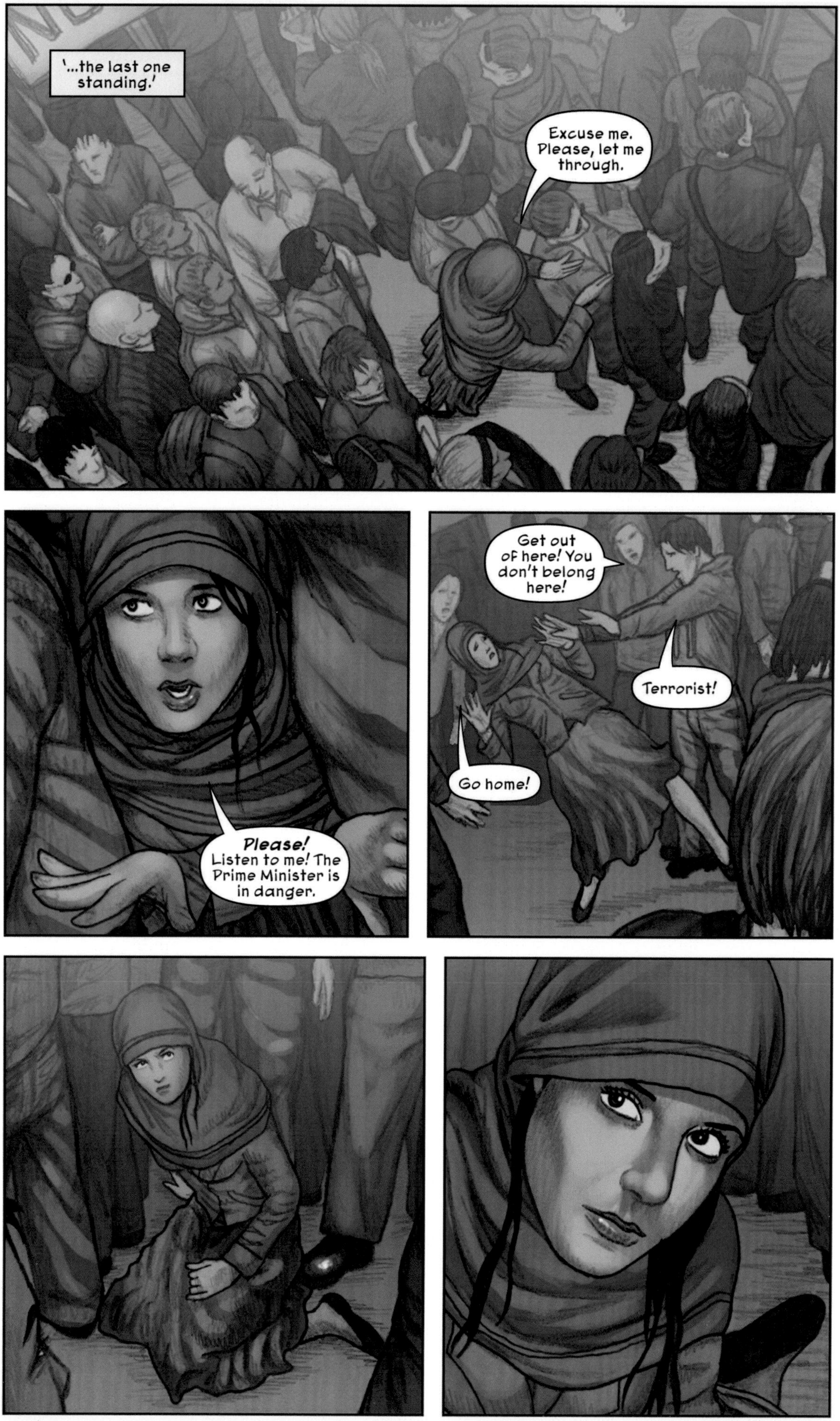
'...the last one standing.'
Excuse me. Please, let me through.
Please! Listen to me! The Prime Minister is in danger.
Get out of here! You don't belong here!
Terrorist!
Go home!

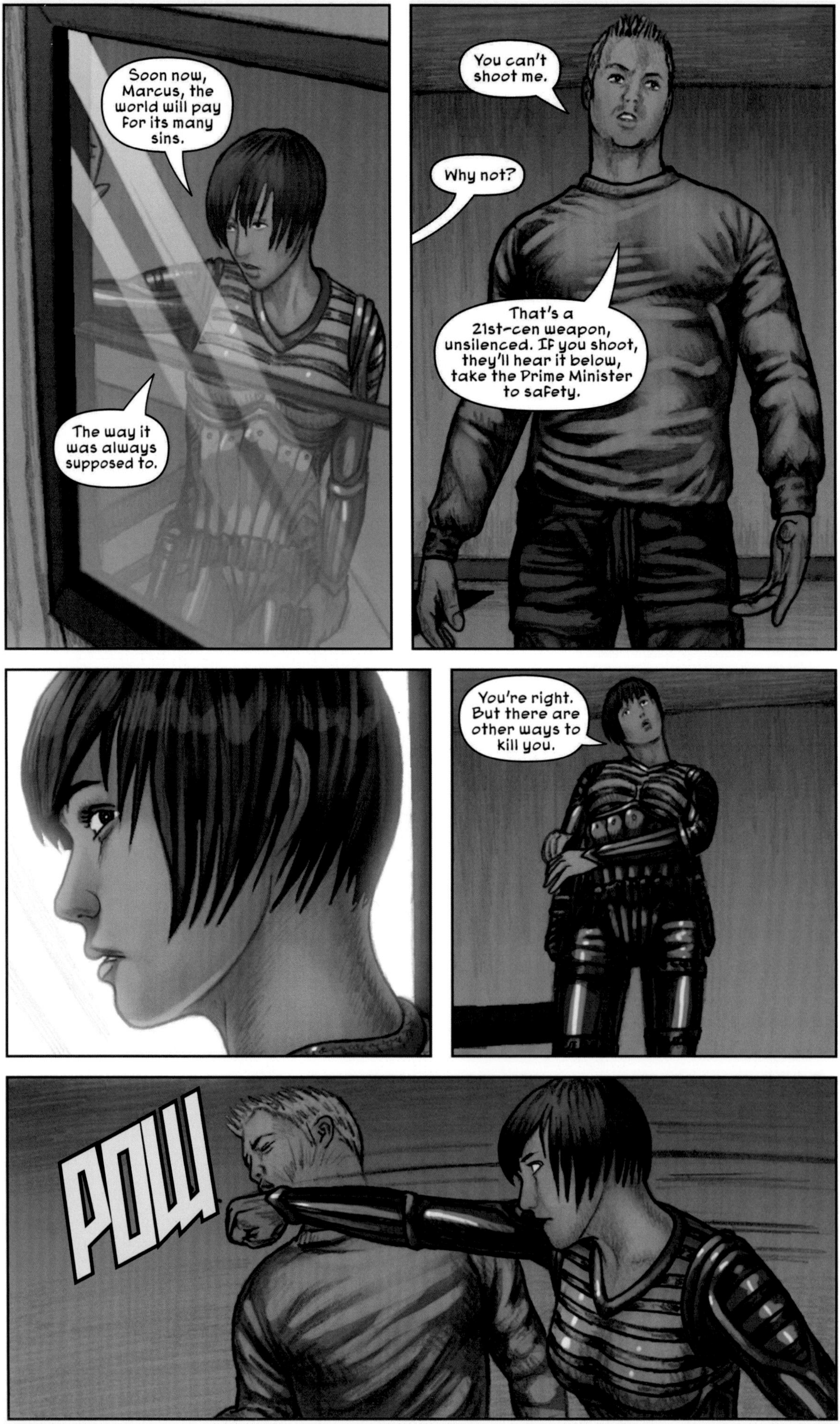
Soon now, Marcus, the world will pay for its many sins.
The way it was always supposed to.
You can't shoot me.
Why not?
That's a 21st-cen weapon, unsilenced. If you shoot, they'll hear it below, take the Prime Minister to safety.
You're right. But there are other ways to kill you.
POW

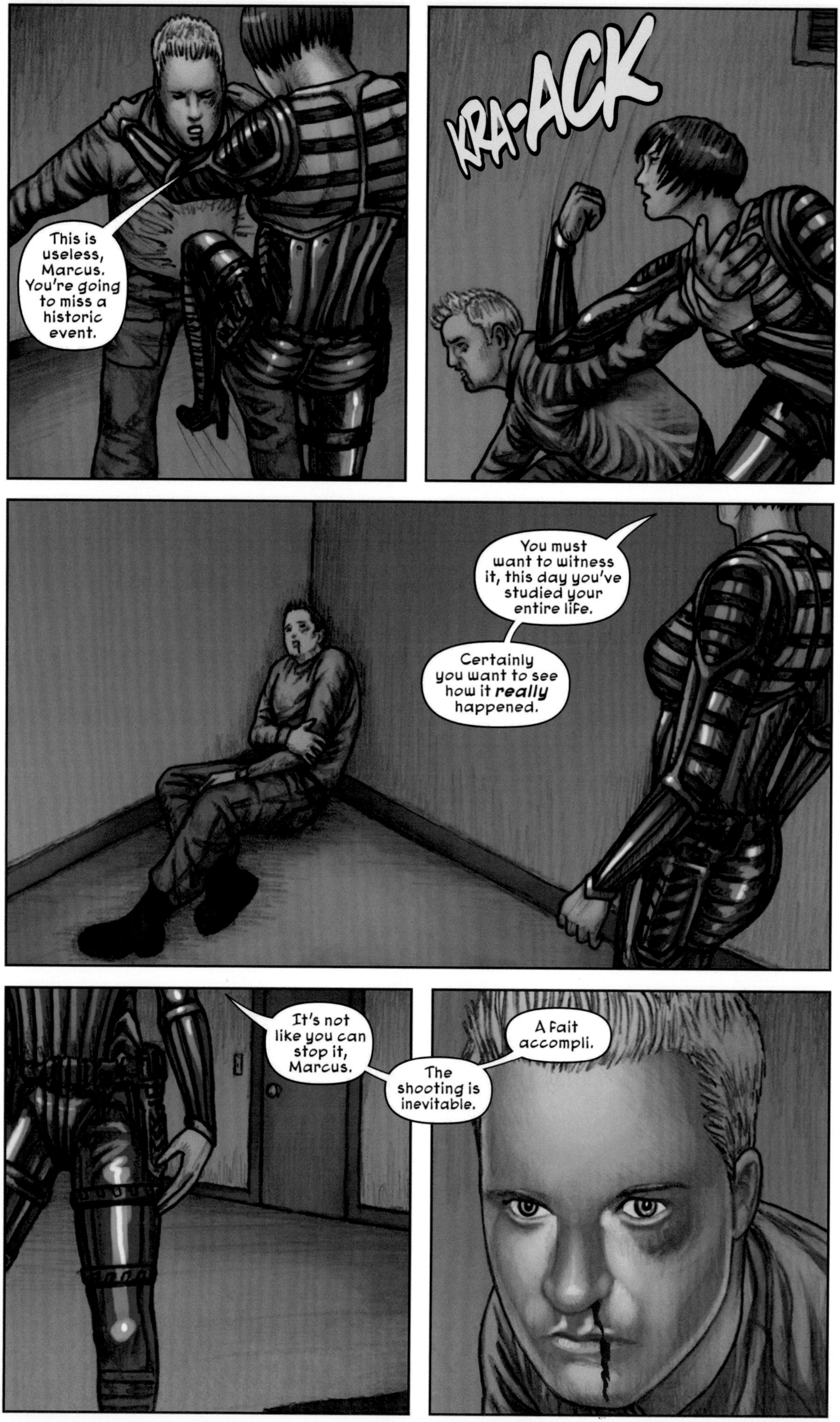
This is useless, Marcus. You're going to miss a historic event.
KRA-ACK
You must want to witness it, this day you've studied your entire life.
Certainly you want to see how it *really* happened.
It's not like you can stop it, Marcus.
The shooting is inevitable.
A fait accompli.

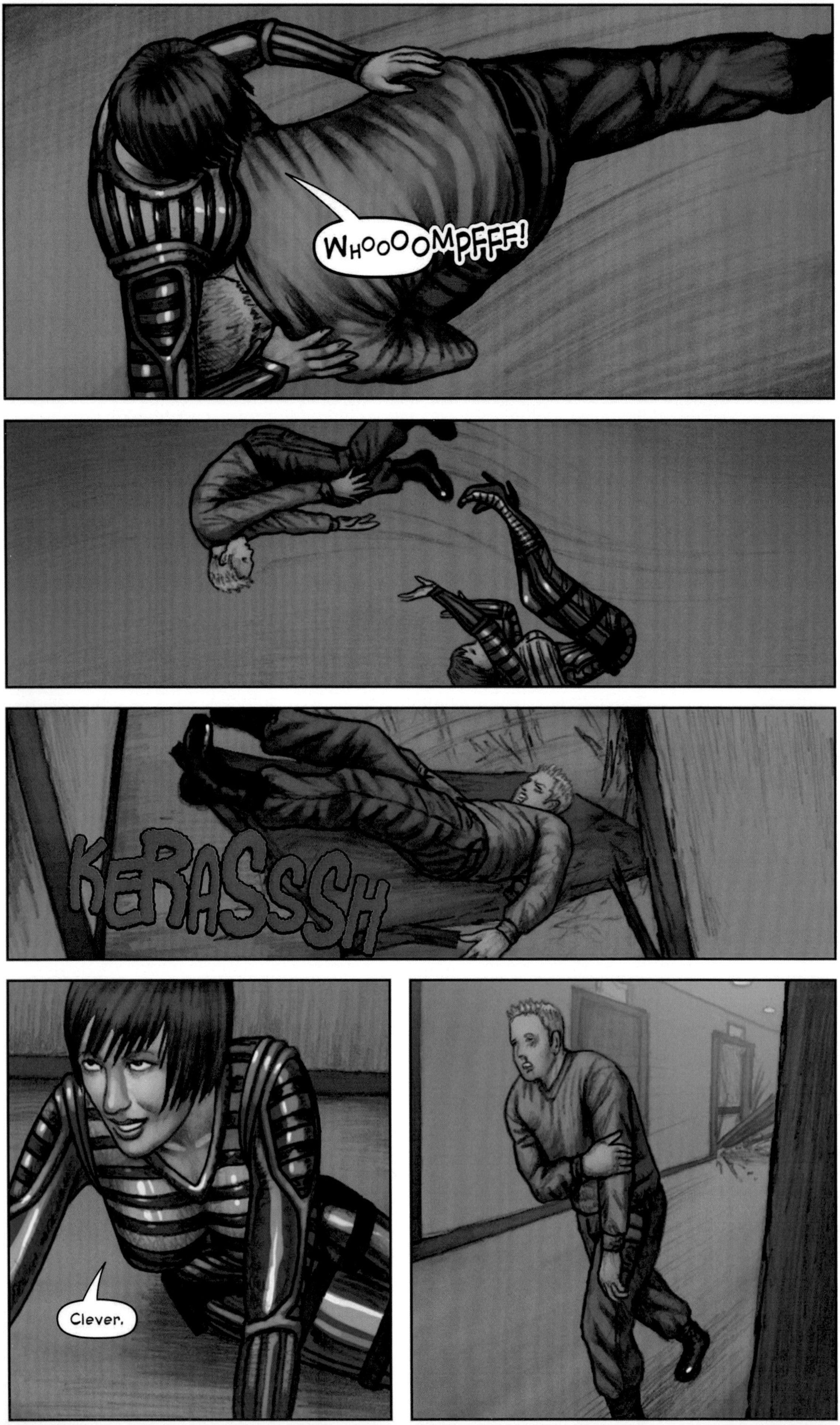
WHOOOOMPFFF!
KERASSSH
Clever.

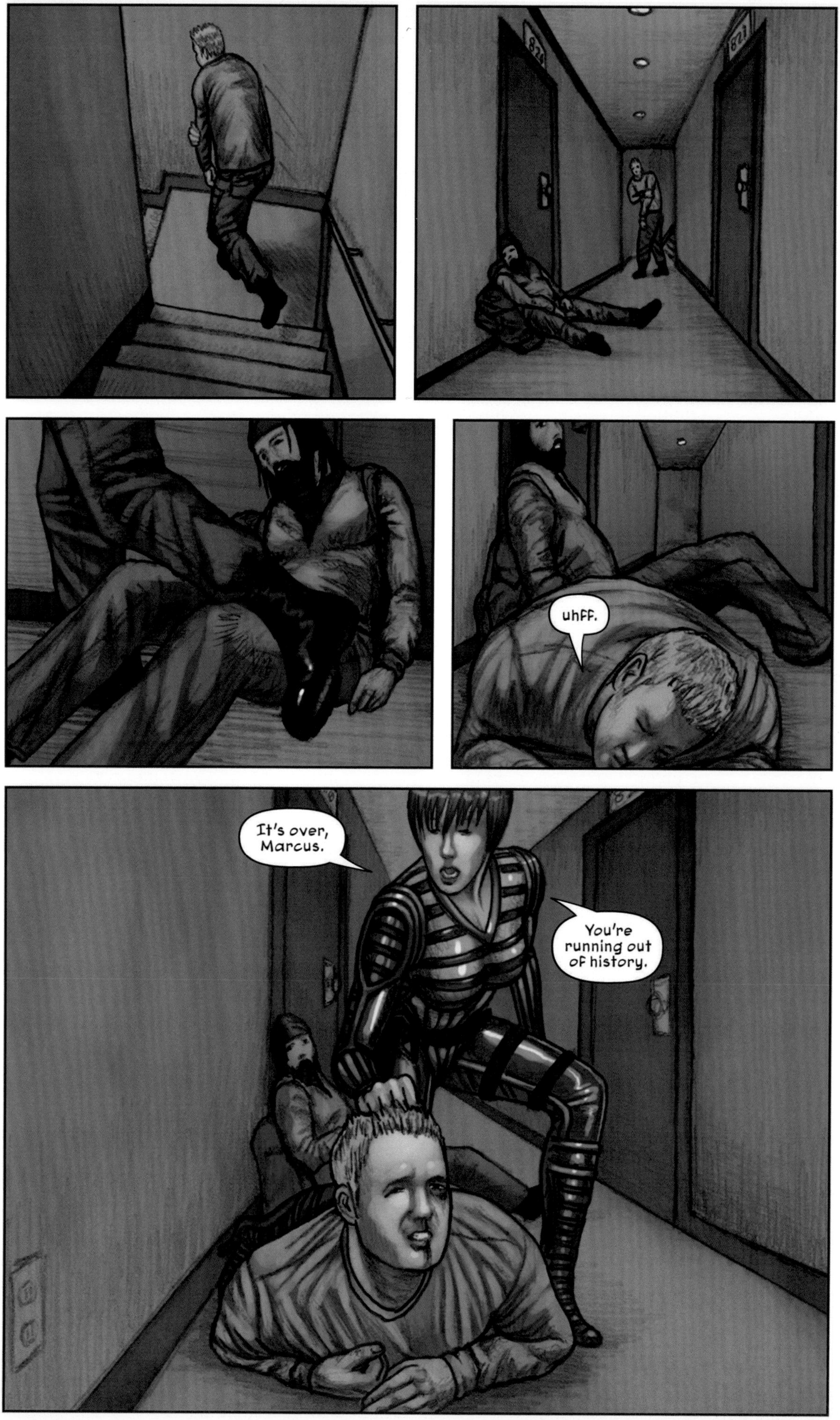
uhff.
It's over, Marcus.
You're running out of history.

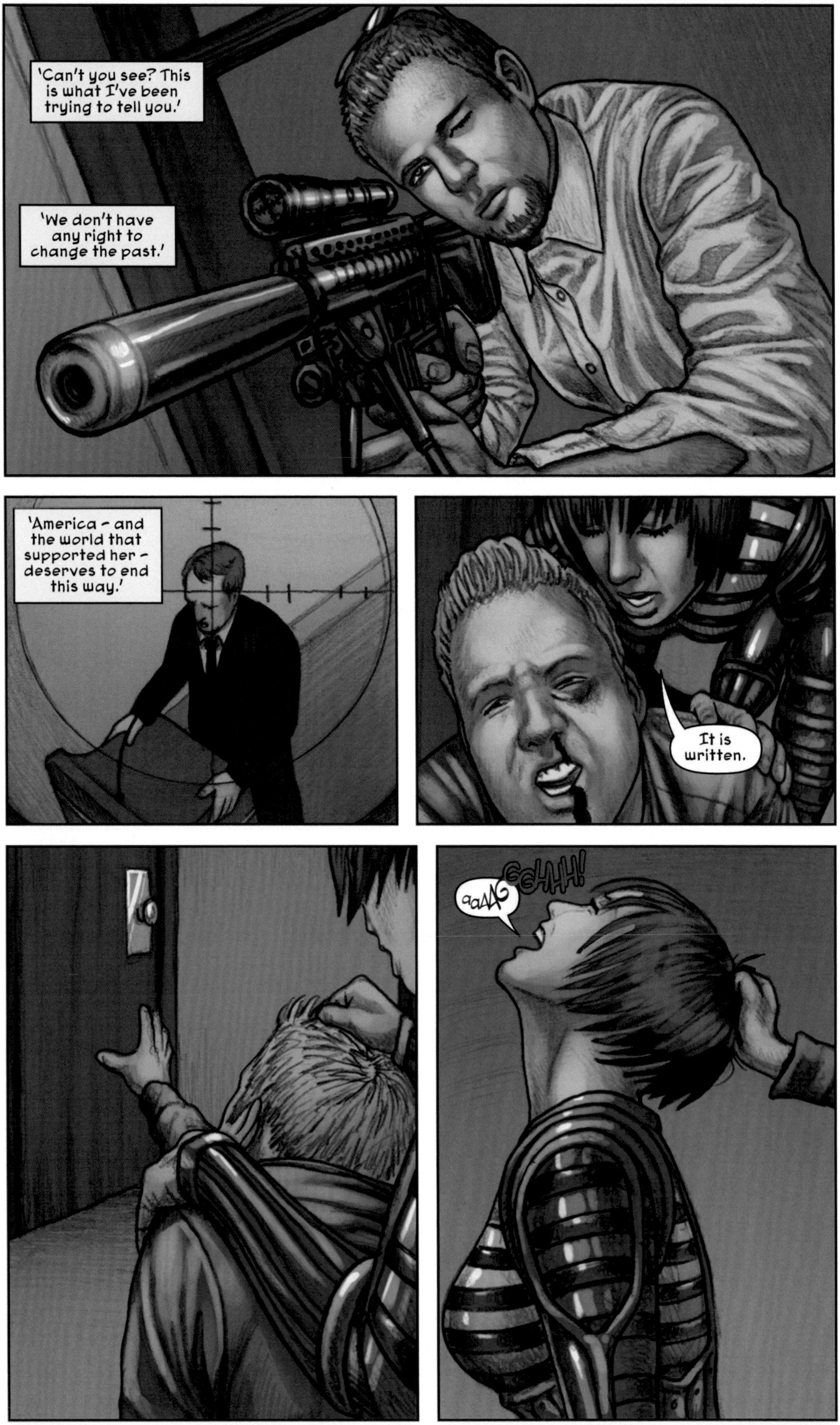
'Can't you see? This is what I've been trying to tell you.'
'We don't have any right to change the past.'
'America - and the world that supported her - deserves to end this way.'
It is written.
aaAAGGGHHH!

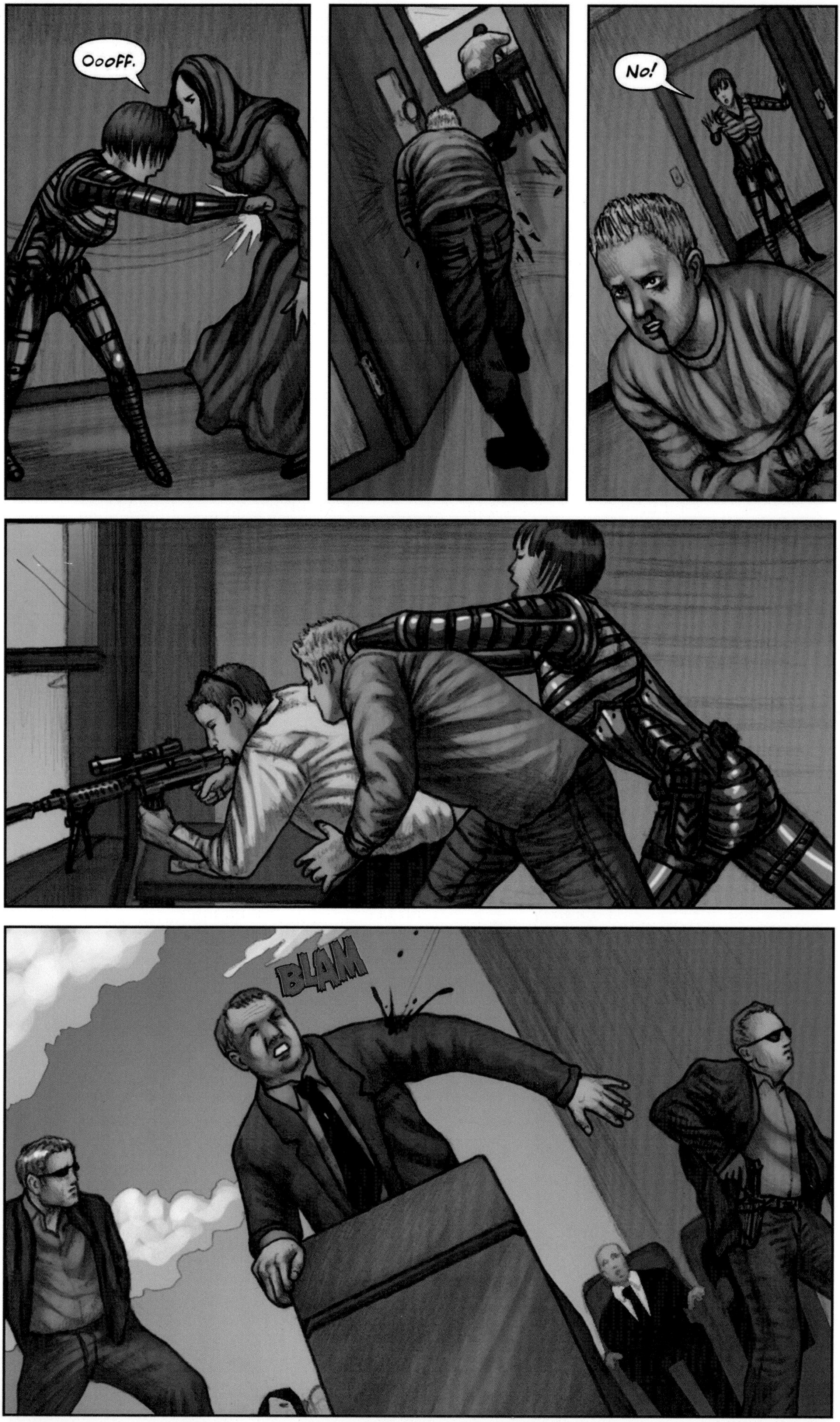
OooFF.
No!
BLAM

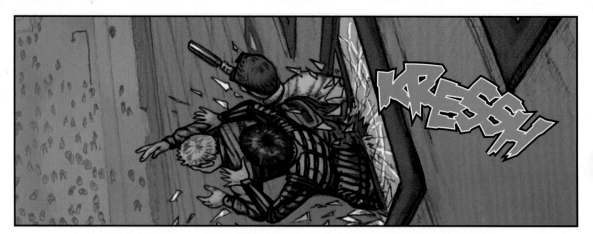

KREEEH

What's happening?

...shot the Prime Minister...

...heard two shots...

Get down!

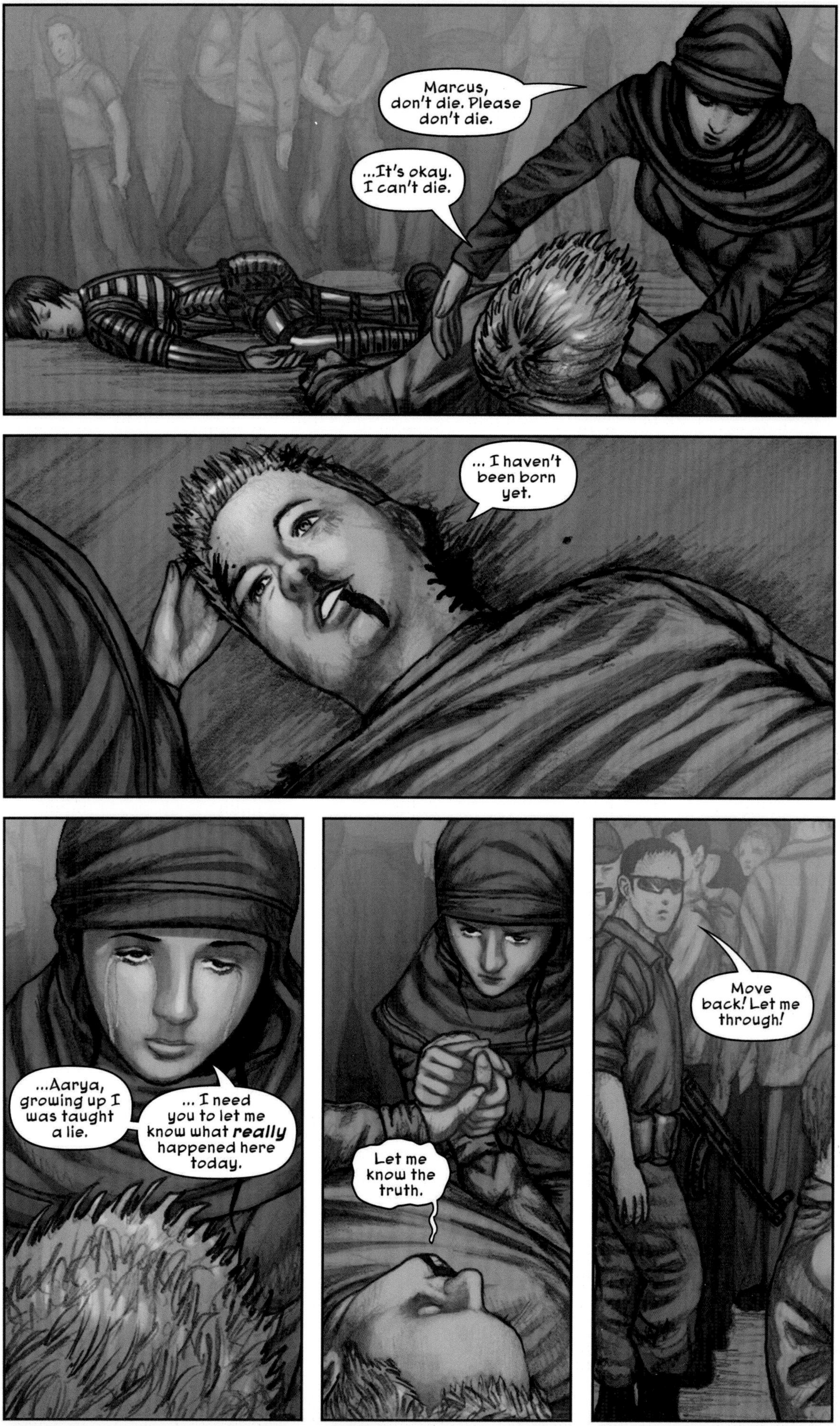
Marcus, don't die. Please don't die.
...It's okay. I can't die.
... I haven't been born yet.
...Aarya, growing up I was taught a lie.
... I need you to let me know what ***really*** happened here today.
Let me know the truth.
Move back! Let me through!

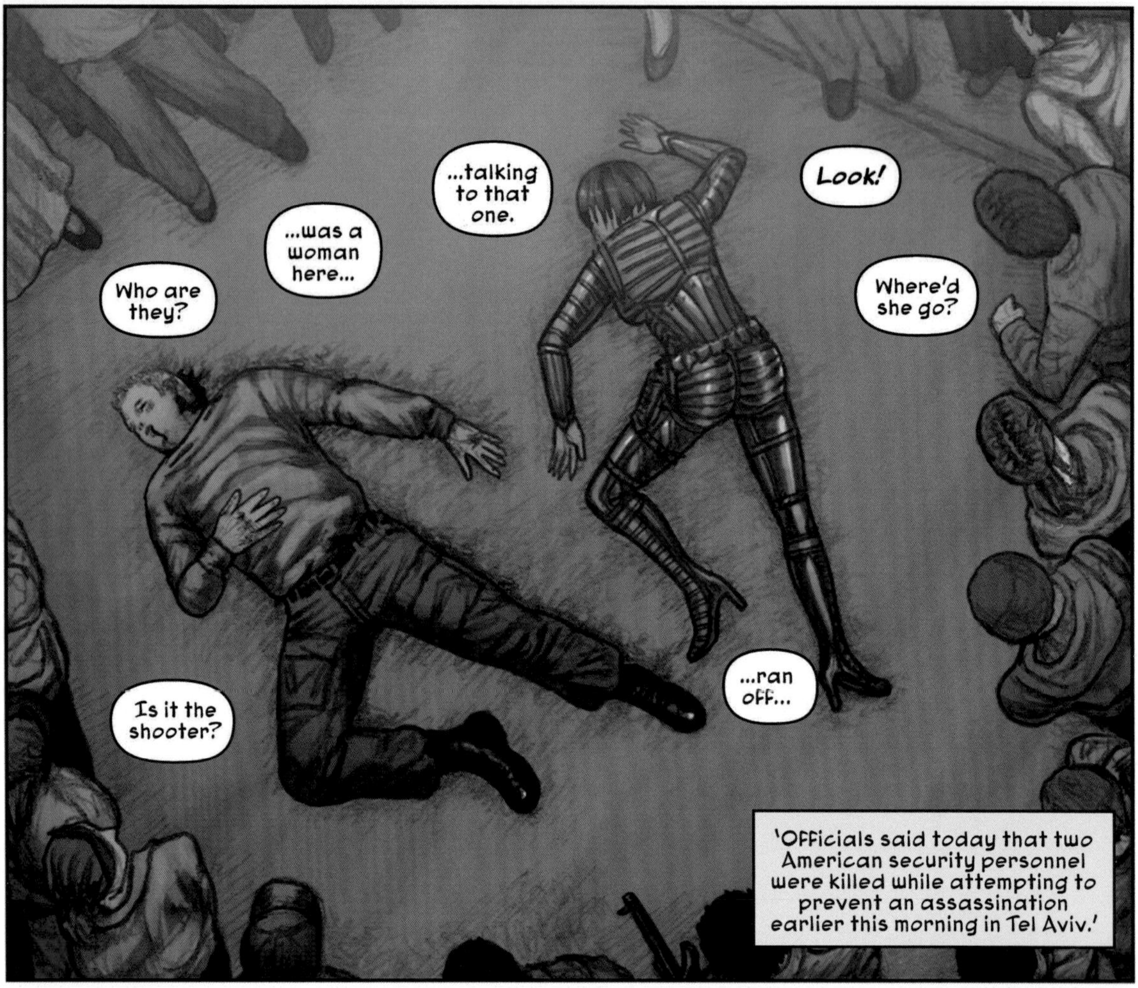
Who are they?
...was a woman here...
...talking to that one.
Look!
Where'd she go?
Is it the shooter?
...ran off...
'Officials said today that two American security personnel were killed while attempting to prevent an assassination earlier this morning in Tel Aviv.'

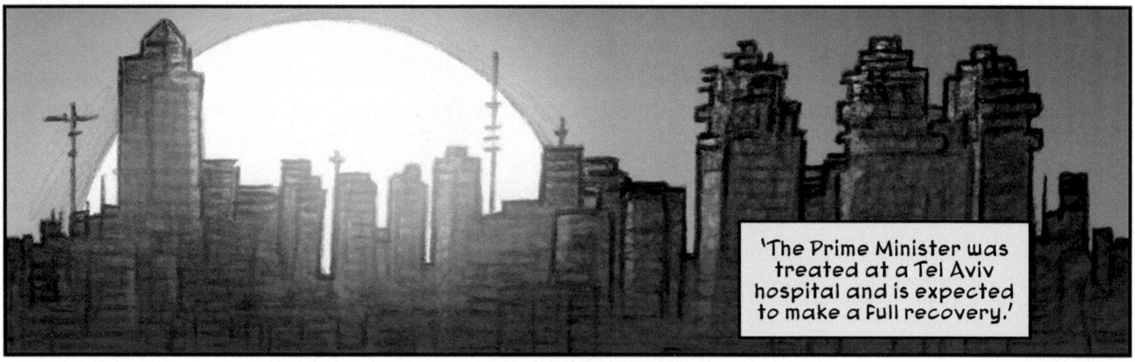
'The Prime Minister was treated at a Tel Aviv hospital and is expected to make a full recovery.'

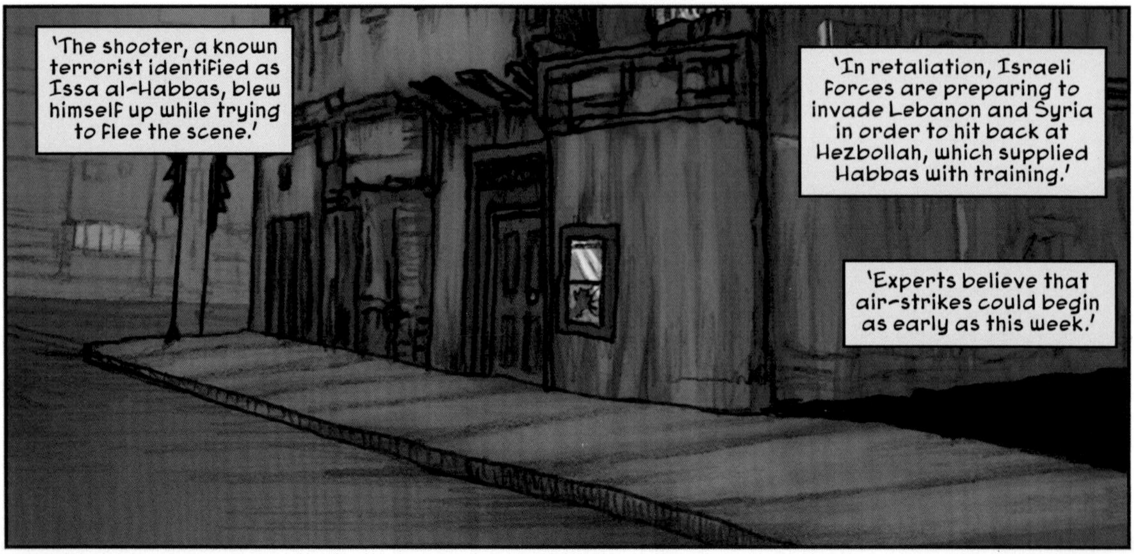
'The shooter, a known terrorist identified as Issa al-Habbas, blew himself up while trying to flee the scene.'
'In retaliation, Israeli forces are preparing to invade Lebanon and Syria in order to hit back at Hezbollah, which supplied Habbas with training.'
'Experts believe that air-strikes could begin as early as this week.'

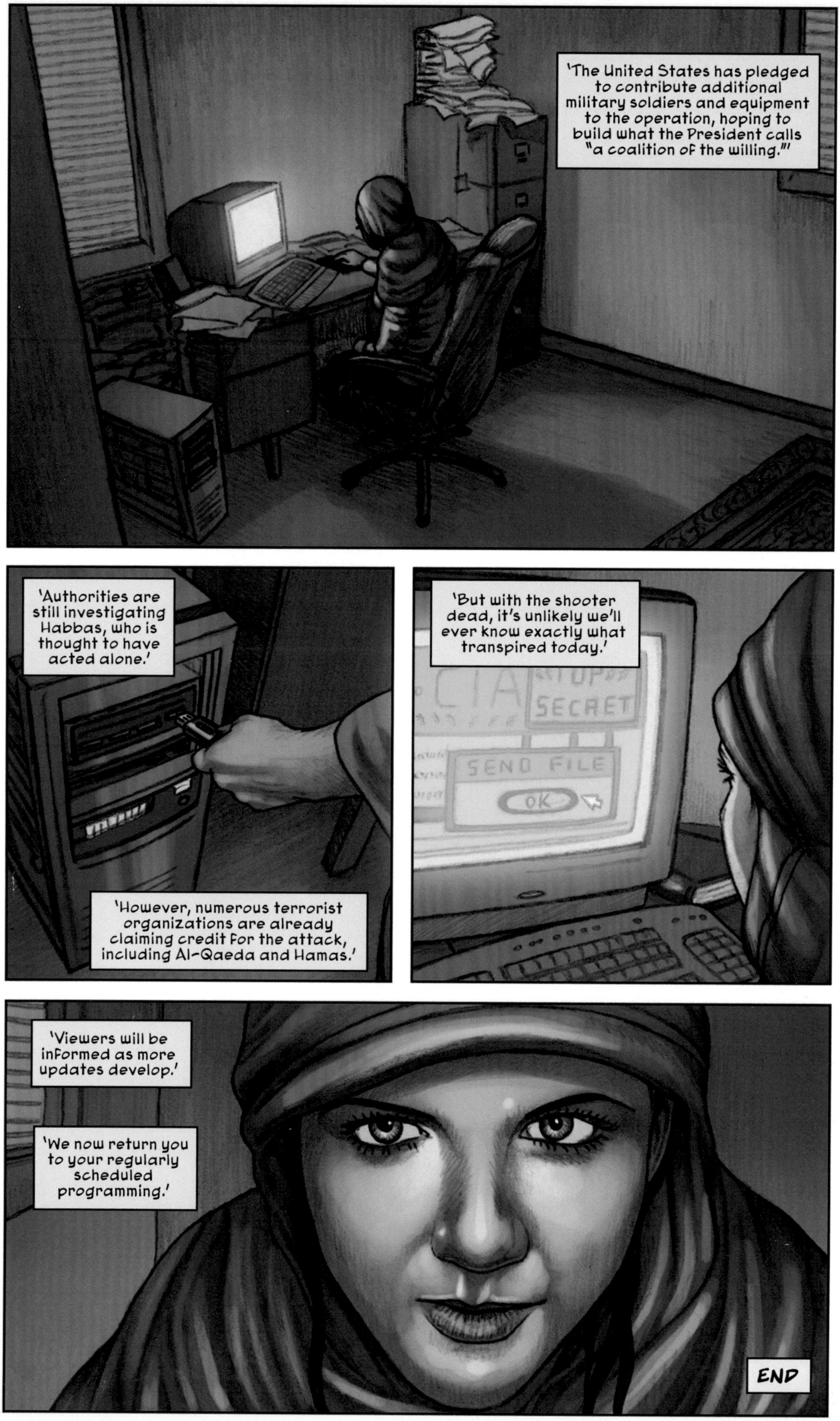
'The United States has pledged to contribute additional military soldiers and equipment to the operation, hoping to build what the President calls "a coalition of the willing."'
'Authorities are still investigating Habbas, who is thought to have acted alone.'
'However, numerous terrorist organizations are already claiming credit for the attack, including Al-Qaeda and Hamas.'
'But with the shooter dead, it's unlikely we'll ever know exactly what transpired today.'
CIA
SECRET
SEND FILE
OK
'Viewers will be informed as more updates develop.'
'We now return you to your regularly scheduled programming.'
END

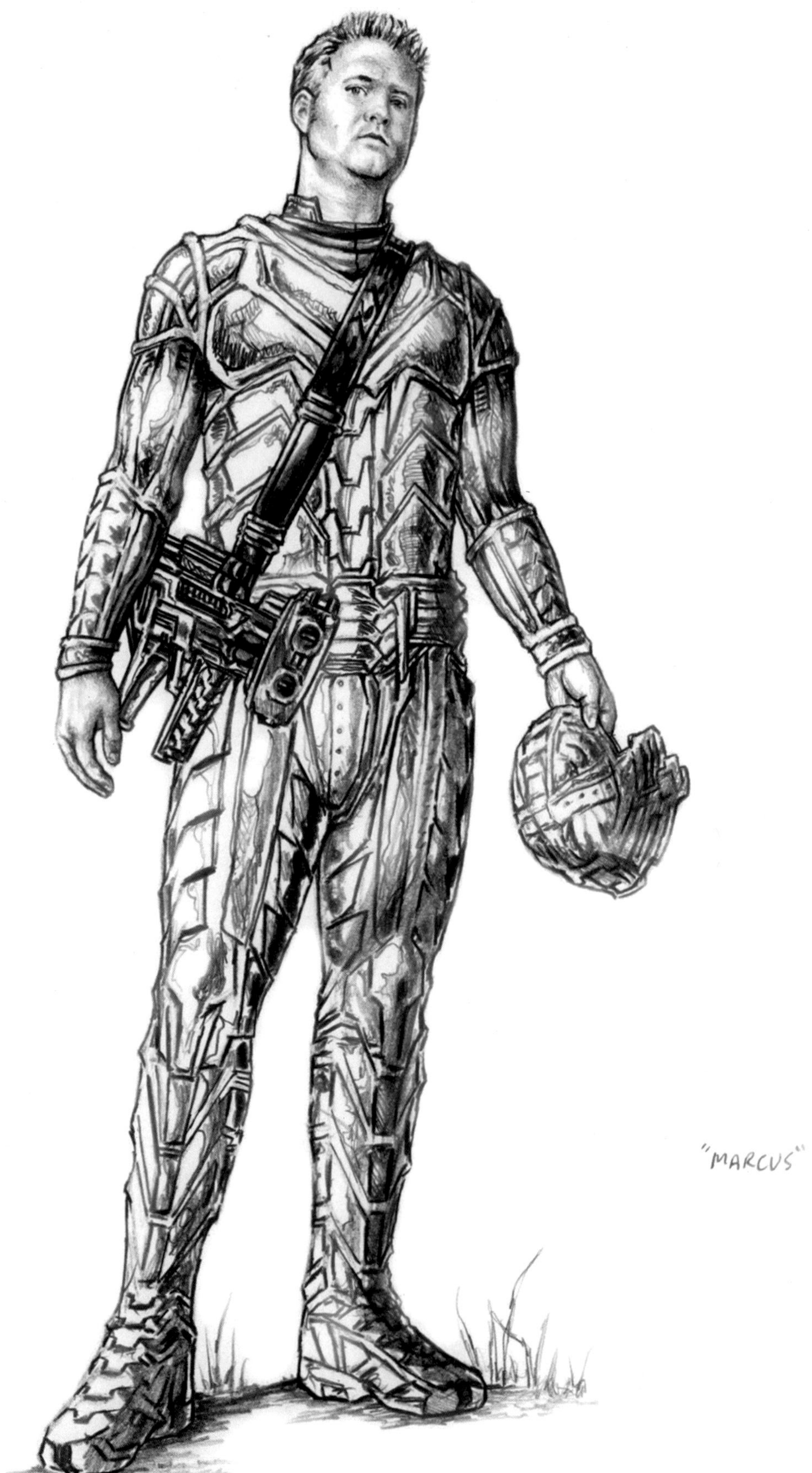
"MARCUS"